TEXT BOOK OF PHYSICAL PHARMACEUTICS-II

VISHESH KUMAR MAURYA

To my family, for their unwavering support and encouragement.

To my mentors and colleagues, whose wisdom and guidance have been invaluable.

To my students, who inspire me to learn and grow every day.

And to the pioneers of pharmaceutical sciences, whose groundbreaking work continues to shape the future of medicine.

This book is dedicated with profound gratitude and respect.

Contents

Foreword

In the ever-evolving field of pharmaceutical sciences, understanding the fundamental principles of physical pharmaceutics is crucial for anyone involved in the development, production, and application of pharmaceutical products. This book aims to bridge the gap between theoretical concepts and practical applications, providing a comprehensive guide to the physical and chemical principles that underpin drug formulation and delivery.

The journey of creating this book has been both challenging and rewarding. The content has been meticulously curated to offer insights into key areas such as solubility, stability, drug delivery systems, and the physical properties of pharmaceuticals. Each chapter is designed to build on the last, offering a progressive understanding of complex topics in a clear and accessible manner.

This book would not have been possible without the contributions of many dedicated professionals. Researchers, educators, and industry experts have all played a part in shaping the content and ensuring its relevance and accuracy. Their collective knowledge and experience have been instrumental in producing a resource that is both informative and practical.

As we stand on the threshold of new advancements in pharmaceutical sciences, it is essential to equip the next generation of pharmacists, researchers, and practitioners with the tools they need to succeed. This book is intended not only as a textbook for students but also as a reference for professionals in the field. It is our hope that it will serve as a valuable resource, inspiring innovation and fostering a deeper understanding of the science behind pharmaceuticals.

We live in a time of rapid scientific advancement, where the possibilities for new therapies and treatments are limited only by our imagination and understanding. By delving into the principles outlined in this book, readers will be better prepared to contribute to the exciting future of pharmaceutical sciences.

Thank you for embarking on this journey with us. We hope this book will enhance your knowledge, inspire your curiosity, and support your endeavors in the fascinating world of physical pharmaceutics.

Vishesh Kumar Maurya
Mohammad Rizwan
Km Reena
Jyoti Chandi
Sofiya Ansari

Preface

The field of physical pharmaceutics is a cornerstone of pharmaceutical sciences, encompassing the study of the physical and chemical properties of drugs and their dosage forms. This book is designed to provide a comprehensive introduction to the principles and applications of physical pharmaceutics, serving as a vital resource for students, researchers, and practitioners in the field.

Over the years, the landscape of pharmaceutical sciences has transformed dramatically, driven by advances in technology, research, and a deeper understanding of the complex interactions between drugs and biological systems. This evolution has underscored the importance of a solid foundation in physical pharmaceutics, as it is essential for the development of safe, effective, and innovative therapeutic solutions.

The goal of this book is to present a balanced blend of theory and practice. Each chapter has been carefully structured to offer clear explanations of fundamental concepts, followed by detailed discussions on their practical applications. Topics such as solubility, dissolution, stability, and drug delivery systems are explored in depth, with a focus on how these principles can be applied in real-world pharmaceutical contexts.

Throughout the writing process, we have drawn on the latest research and developments in the field, incorporating contemporary examples and case studies to illustrate key points. Our aim is to make complex subjects accessible and engaging, fostering a deeper understanding and appreciation of physical pharmaceutics.

This book is the result of collaboration and contributions from many individuals. We extend our heartfelt thanks to our colleagues and peers who have shared their expertise and insights. Their invaluable feedback has helped shape the content and ensure its relevance and accuracy.

We also express our gratitude to the students who have used earlier drafts of this book in their studies. Their questions, comments, and enthusiasm have been a source of inspiration, driving us to refine and improve the material.

As you delve into the chapters ahead, we hope you find this book to be a useful and enlightening resource. Whether you are a student beginning your journey in pharmaceutical sciences or a seasoned professional seeking to deepen your knowledge, our aim is to provide you with the tools and understanding necessary to excel in this dynamic and vital field.

Thank you for choosing this book. We look forward to accompanying you on your path to discovery and innovation in physical pharmaceutics.

Vishesh Kumar Maurya
Mohammad Rizwan
Km Reena
Jyoti Chandi
Sofiya Ansari

Acknowledgements

The creation of this book has been a collaborative journey, and it is with deep gratitude that I acknowledge the contributions of those who have made it possible.

First and foremost, I would like to thank my family for their unwavering support and encouragement throughout this project. Your patience, understanding, and love have been my greatest source of strength.

To my mentors and colleagues, your wisdom and guidance have been invaluable. Your insights and feedback have helped shape the direction and content of this book, ensuring its accuracy and relevance.

I extend my heartfelt thanks to **Mohammad Rizwan , Km Reena , Jyoti Chandi , Sofiya Ansari** who have engaged with the early drafts of this book. Your questions, comments, and enthusiasm have driven me to refine and improve the material. Your dedication to learning has been a constant source of motivation.

Special thanks go to the peer reviewers and editors who have meticulously examined the manuscript. Your critical eye and thoughtful suggestions have greatly enhanced the clarity and quality of this work. I am particularly indebted to for your exceptional editorial skills and dedication.

I am also grateful to my colleagues and collaborators in the pharmaceutical sciences community. Your contributions, whether through direct collaboration or inspiring research, have enriched the content of this book. I would like to acknowledge the support for providing the resources and environment conducive to this work.

To the pioneers of pharmaceutical sciences, whose groundbreaking work has laid the foundation for this field,

I owe a debt of gratitude. Your discoveries and innovations continue to inspire and guide us.

Finally, I would like to thank the publishing team for their professionalism and support throughout the publication process. Your expertise and dedication have been crucial in bringing this book to fruition.

This book is a testament to the collective efforts of many individuals, and it is with sincere appreciation that I acknowledge each one of you. Thank you for your contributions, support, and belief in this project.

Prologue

Colloidal Dispersions:

Introduction to Colloidal Dispersions

Colloidal dispersions are mixtures where one substance (the dispersed phase) is evenly distributed in another substance (the continuous phase). The dispersed particles are typically in the range of 1 to 1000 nanometers, larger than molecules but small enough to remain suspended without settling out due to gravity. These systems are ubiquitous in nature and industry, found in products as diverse as milk, paint, fog, and blood.

Types of Colloidal Dispersions

Colloidal dispersions can be categorized based on the states of the dispersed and continuous phases:

1. **Sols**: Solid particles in a liquid, such as paints and inks.
2. **Gels**: Liquid particles in a solid, like jelly and gelatin.
3. **Emulsions**: Liquid particles in another liquid, for instance, mayonnaise and milk.
4. **Foams**: Gas particles in a liquid or solid, seen in whipped cream and styrofoam.
5. **Aerosols**: Solid or liquid particles in a gas, such as smoke and fog.

Properties of Colloidal Dispersions

Colloids exhibit unique properties due to their size and the interaction between the dispersed and continuous phases:

- **Brownian Motion**: The dispersed particles undergo random motion due to collisions with the molecules of the continuous phase. This motion helps keep the particles suspended.

- **Tyndall Effect**: Colloidal dispersions scatter light, making a beam of light visible as it passes through the mixture. This phenomenon is used to distinguish colloids from true solutions.
- **Electrophoresis**: When subjected to an electric field, charged colloidal particles move towards the electrode of opposite charge. This property is exploited in techniques like gel electrophoresis for DNA separation.
- **Stability**: Colloidal particles tend to remain evenly distributed due to repulsive forces between them, preventing aggregation. Stabilizing agents, like surfactants or polymers, can be added to enhance stability.

Applications of Colloidal Dispersions

Colloidal dispersions play critical roles in various industries and everyday products:

- **Food Industry**: Many foods are colloids, such as milk, butter, and salad dressings. The texture, appearance, and stability of these products rely on their colloidal nature.
- **Pharmaceuticals**: Colloidal systems are used in drug delivery, where nanoparticles can enhance the solubility and bioavailability of drugs.
- **Cosmetics**: Creams, lotions, and sunscreens often involve colloidal dispersions to ensure even application and absorption.
- **Environmental Science**: Colloidal suspensions are used in water purification processes to remove contaminants.
- **Materials Science**: Colloidal processing is crucial in the

fabrication of ceramics, inks, and coatings.

Stability and Control of Colloidal Dispersions

Ensuring the stability of colloidal dispersions is essential for their practical use. Instability can arise from aggregation or sedimentation of the dispersed particles. Several factors and techniques are employed to maintain and control colloidal stability:

- **Electrostatic Stabilization**: Charged particles repel each other, preventing aggregation. This is often controlled by adjusting the pH or ionic strength of the medium.
- **Steric Stabilization**: Polymers adsorbed on the surface of colloidal particles create a physical barrier that hinders close approach and aggregation.
- **Surfactants**: These molecules contain both hydrophilic and hydrophobic parts, reducing surface tension and stabilizing emulsions and foams.
- **Shear Forces**: Applying mechanical forces, like stirring or shaking, can help distribute particles evenly and prevent settling.

Challenges and Future Directions

Despite their wide applications, colloidal dispersions pose challenges, including:

- **Stability Control**: Achieving long-term stability can be difficult, especially in varying environmental conditions.
- **Characterization**: Understanding the precise nature of colloidal particles and their interactions requires sophisticated techniques like dynamic light scattering (DLS) and electron microscopy.

- **Scalability**: Producing colloidal dispersions on an industrial scale while maintaining consistency and quality is a significant challenge.

Future research aims to develop smart colloidal systems that respond to environmental stimuli, enhancing their functionality and expanding their applications in fields like medicine, environmental science, and nanotechnology.

Classification of Colloids

Colloids can be classified based on different criteria such as the physical state of the dispersed phase and the dispersion medium, the nature of the interaction between the dispersed phase and the dispersion medium, and the type of particles involved.

1. **Based on Physical State**:

   - **Sol**: Solid particles in a liquid (e.g., paint, ink).
   - **Gel**: Liquid particles in a solid (e.g., jelly, gelatin).
   - **Emulsion**: Liquid particles in another liquid (e.g., milk, mayonnaise).
   - **Foam**: Gas particles in a liquid or solid (e.g., whipped cream, styrofoam).
   - **Aerosol**: Solid or liquid particles in a gas (e.g., smoke, fog).

2. **Based on Interaction**:

   - **Lyophilic Colloids (Solvent-loving)**: These colloids have a strong affinity between the dispersed phase and the dispersion medium (e.g., gum, gelatin in water).

- **Lyophobic Colloids (Solvent-hating)**: These colloids have little to no affinity between the dispersed phase and the dispersion medium (e.g., gold sol, arsenic sulfide sol).

3. **Based on Particle Type**:

   - **Multimolecular Colloids**: Aggregates of many atoms or molecules (e.g., sulfur sol).
   - **Macromolecular Colloids**: Large molecules dispersed in a medium (e.g., starch, proteins).
   - **Associated Colloids (Micelles)**: Colloids that form at higher concentrations where molecules aggregate into micelles (e.g., soaps and detergents).

Comparative Account of General Properties
Optical Properties

1. **Tyndall Effect**:

   - Colloidal dispersions scatter light when a beam is passed through them, making the path of the light visible. This effect distinguishes colloids from true solutions.
   - **Example**: The visibility of light beams in fog or dusty air.

2. **Color**:

   - The color of colloidal dispersions depends on the size and nature of the particles as well as the wavelength of the light scattered.
   - **Example**: Gold sol appears red or purple depending

on particle size.

Kinetic Properties

1. **Brownian Motion**:

   - The random, zigzag motion of colloidal particles due to collisions with molecules of the dispersion medium.
   - **Importance**: Helps keep particles dispersed and prevents settling.

2. **Diffusion**:

   - Colloidal particles diffuse from regions of higher concentration to regions of lower concentration, but more slowly compared to smaller molecules due to their larger size.

3. **Sedimentation**:

   - Due to their small size, colloidal particles do not settle under gravity over time; they exhibit very slow sedimentation.
   - **Exception**: Ultracentrifugation can accelerate sedimentation for colloidal particles.

Electrical Properties

1. **Electrophoresis**:

   - When subjected to an electric field, charged colloidal particles move towards the electrode of opposite charge. This movement helps determine the charge and mobility of particles.

- **Application**: Gel electrophoresis for separating DNA or proteins.

2. **Electro-osmosis**:

- The movement of the dispersion medium relative to the stationary colloidal particles under the influence of an electric field.
- **Relevance**: Important in understanding the behavior of colloids in porous materials and biological tissues.

3. **Charge and Stability**:

- Colloidal particles often acquire charges by ionization or adsorption of ions, leading to the formation of an electrical double layer around each particle. The repulsion between similarly charged particles helps in stabilizing the colloid.
- **Example**: Stability of colloidal gold is due to the negative charge on gold particles.

Effects of Electrolytes, Coacervation, Peptization, and Protective Action in Colloidal Dispersions

Colloidal dispersions are intricate systems with particles finely distributed within a continuous phase. The behavior and stability of these dispersions can be influenced by various factors, including the presence of electrolytes, coacervation, peptization, and protective actions. Understanding these concepts is crucial for manipulating and optimizing colloidal systems in various applications.

Effect of Electrolytes

Electrolytes, when added to a colloidal dispersion, can significantly alter its stability. The presence of ions affects the electrostatic interactions between colloidal particles. The effects of electrolytes can be categorized into:

1. **Coagulation and Flocculation:**

   - **Coagulation:** The addition of electrolytes can neutralize the surface charges on colloidal particles, reducing the repulsive forces that keep them apart. When the repulsive barrier is diminished, particles can come closer and aggregate, leading to coagulation. The coagulation threshold depends on the valency of the ions; multivalent ions are more effective in causing coagulation than monovalent ions (Schulze-Hardy rule).
   - **Flocculation:** In some cases, electrolytes cause particles to form loose aggregates (flocs) that can be easily separated from the dispersion. This is particularly useful in water treatment processes.

1. **Stabilization:**

   - **Stabilizing Effect:** At low concentrations, certain electrolytes can stabilize colloids by compressing the electrical double layer around the particles, thus preventing close contact and aggregation. This can enhance the dispersion's stability against flocculation.

Coacervation

Coacervation is a phase separation process where a colloidal solution separates into two liquid phases: a dense coacervate phase and a dilute supernatant phase. This phenomenon is driven by changes in conditions such as pH, temperature, or the addition of a non-solvent. Coacervation can be classified into:

1. **Simple Coacervation**:

   - This occurs when a single colloid is involved. A change in conditions leads to the formation of coacervate droplets, which can encapsulate other substances. Simple coacervation is often used in microencapsulation technologies.

2. **Complex Coacervation**:

   - This involves interactions between two oppositely charged colloids, such as proteins and polysaccharides. The resulting electrostatic attraction leads to the formation of a coacervate phase, which can be used to create complex microstructures and delivery systems.

   Peptization

   Peptization is the process of converting a coagulated or flocculated precipitate back into a stable colloidal dispersion by adding a peptizing agent. The peptizing agent, often a suitable electrolyte, adsorbs onto the surface of the precipitate particles, imparting charge and dispersing them into the continuous phase. This process is crucial in:

1. **Reversing Coagulation**:

- After coagulation, peptization can restore the original colloidal state, allowing for further processing or utilization of the colloid.

2. **Industrial Applications**:

   - Peptization is essential in industries like ceramics and pharmaceuticals, where controlled dispersion and re-dispersion of particles are required.

Protective Action

Protective action refers to the stabilization of colloidal particles by the addition of a protective colloid, often a polymer or surfactant, which adsorbs onto the particle surface and prevents aggregation. This action can be explained through:

1. **Steric Stabilization**:

   - Protective colloids create a physical barrier around colloidal particles, preventing them from coming close enough to aggregate. The adsorbed layers provide steric hindrance, which is particularly effective in non-aqueous systems.

2. **Electrostatic Stabilization**:

   - Some protective colloids also impart additional surface charge, enhancing the electrostatic repulsion between particles. This dual mechanism (steric and electrostatic) offers robust stabilization in various media.

3. **Industrial and Biological Relevance**:

   - Protective action is vital in formulating stable emulsions, foams, and suspensions in the food, cosmetics, and pharmaceutical industries. In biological systems, naturally occurring protective colloids like proteins and polysaccharides maintain the stability of cellular components and bodily fluids.

Rheology: Understanding the Flow of Matter
Introduction to Rheology

Rheology is the science of deformation and flow of matter. It explores how materials respond to applied forces, encompassing both solids and liquids. While solids typically exhibit elasticity and liquids display viscosity, rheology investigates materials that exhibit characteristics of both, such as gels, pastes, and polymers.

Historical Background

The term "rheology" was coined in the 1920s by Eugene C. Bingham, a professor at Lafayette College, and Markus Reiner, an Israeli scientist. It stems from the Greek word "rheo," meaning "to flow," and "logia," meaning "the study of." Rheology has its roots in classical mechanics but has since evolved to incorporate modern techniques and theories.

Fundamental Concepts

1. **Viscosity**:

   - **Definition**: Viscosity is a measure of a fluid's resistance to flow. It's the internal friction within the fluid that resists deformation.
   - **Newtonian vs. Non-Newtonian Fluids**: Newtonian

fluids have a constant viscosity regardless of the applied shear rate (e.g., water, air). Non-Newtonian fluids exhibit a variable viscosity depending on the shear rate or shear history (e.g., ketchup, blood).

2. **Elasticity**:

   - **Definition**: Elasticity describes a material's ability to return to its original shape after a deforming force is removed.
   - **Elastic Moduli**: Key parameters include Young's modulus (tensile elasticity), shear modulus (response to shear stress), and bulk modulus (response to uniform pressure).

3. **Viscoelasticity**:

   - **Definition**: Viscoelastic materials exhibit both viscous and elastic characteristics. These materials, such as polymers and biological tissues, display time-dependent strain.
   - **Models**: Common models used to describe viscoelastic behavior include the Maxwell model (fluid-like behavior) and the Kelvin-Voigt model (solid-like behavior).

Measurement Techniques

Rheological properties are measured using various instruments:

1. **Rotational Rheometers**:

   - These devices measure the torque and angular

displacement to determine viscosity and viscoelastic properties. They are used for both steady shear and oscillatory tests.

2. **Capillary Rheometers**:

   - These measure the flow of material through a narrow capillary to determine viscosity, particularly useful for high-shear-rate applications like polymer melts.

3. **Dynamic Mechanical Analyzers (DMA)**:

   - DMA applies oscillatory stress or strain and measures the resulting material response, providing insights into viscoelastic behavior.

Applications of Rheology

1. **Industrial Processes**:

   - Rheology is critical in industries such as food processing, pharmaceuticals, cosmetics, and petrochemicals. It helps in optimizing formulations, ensuring product consistency, and enhancing process efficiency.

2. **Material Science**:

   - Understanding the rheological properties of polymers, composites, and other materials aids in the design and development of new materials with desired mechanical properties.

3. **Biological Systems**:

   - Rheology plays a role in understanding the flow properties of biological fluids (e.g., blood, mucus) and the mechanical behavior of tissues, which is crucial for medical diagnostics and treatment.

4. **Geophysics**:

   - The study of the rheological properties of geological materials, such as magma and ice, helps in predicting natural phenomena like volcanic eruptions and glacier movements.

Challenges and Future Directions

Despite significant advancements, rheology faces challenges in understanding complex fluids and materials under extreme conditions. Future research aims to:

1. **Develop Advanced Measurement Techniques**:

   - Innovations in rheometry and imaging techniques will enhance the ability to study materials at micro and nanoscale levels.

2. **Integrate Multiscale Modeling**:

   - Combining rheological measurements with computational models will provide a deeper understanding of material behavior from molecular to macroscopic scales.

3. **Explore New Materials**:

- Research into smart materials, biopolymers, and nanocomposites will expand the applications of rheology in emerging fields.

Newtonian Systems: An Overview

Introduction to Newtonian Systems

Newtonian systems refer to fluids whose viscosity remains constant regardless of the applied shear rate or stress. These fluids follow Newton's law of viscosity, which states that the shear stress between adjacent fluid layers is directly proportional to the rate of change of velocity (shear rate) in the direction perpendicular to the layers. The proportionality constant is the fluid's viscosity.

Newton's Law of Flow

Newton's law of flow can be mathematically expressed as:

$$?=?·?` \tau=\eta·\dot{\gamma}$$

Where:

- $?\tau$ is the shear stress (force per unit area) acting on the fluid.
- $?\eta$ is the dynamic viscosity of the fluid, a measure of its resistance to shear flow.
- $?`\dot{\gamma}$ is the shear rate (the rate at which adjacent layers of fluid move with respect to each other).

In a Newtonian fluid, the viscosity $?\eta$ is a constant, meaning it does not change with varying shear rates. This linear relationship simplifies the analysis and prediction of fluid flow behavior in many engineering applications.

Kinematic Viscosity

Kinematic viscosity ($?v$) is another important property of fluids, defined as the ratio of dynamic viscosity ($?\eta$) to the fluid's density ($?\rho$):

$$?=??v=\rho\eta$$

Kinematic viscosity has units of m2/sm2/s in the SI system and is often used in fluid dynamics calculations where the density of the fluid is an important factor. It provides a measure of the fluid's resistance to flow under the influence of gravity and is crucial in understanding the flow characteristics of fluids in various contexts, such as lubrication, aerodynamics, and hydrodynamics.

Effect of Temperature on Viscosity

The viscosity of fluids is significantly affected by temperature. For Newtonian fluids, the relationship between viscosity and temperature can be described by the following general trends:

1. **Liquids**:

   - As temperature increases, the viscosity of liquids decreases. This is because higher temperatures provide more thermal energy to the molecules, reducing intermolecular attractions and allowing the molecules to move more freely.
   - For many liquids, this relationship can be modeled using an exponential decay function, such as the Arrhenius equation: $?=?\exp(???)\eta=A\exp(RTE)$ Where:

     - $?A$ is a pre-exponential factor.
     - $?E$ is the activation energy for flow.
     - $?R$ is the universal gas constant.
     - $?T$ is the absolute temperature.

2. **Gases**:

- In contrast to liquids, the viscosity of gases increases with temperature. Higher temperatures result in more energetic collisions between gas molecules, increasing the momentum transfer and, consequently, the viscosity.
- For gases, the Sutherland's formula provides a good approximation of the temperature dependence of viscosity: ?=?0(??0)3/2(?0+??+?)$\eta=\eta 0(T0T)3/2(T+CT0+C)$ Where:

  - ?0$\eta 0$ is the reference viscosity at temperature ?0$T0$.
  - ?C is the Sutherland constant, specific to each gas.

Applications and Importance

Understanding the behavior of Newtonian fluids under varying conditions is essential in numerous engineering and scientific fields:

1. **Industrial Processes**:

- Accurate prediction of fluid flow is crucial for designing and optimizing processes in chemical engineering, petroleum engineering, and food processing.

2. **Lubrication**:

- The design of lubrication systems relies on knowledge of the kinematic viscosity of oils, which ensures the proper functioning of machinery by reducing friction and wear.

3. **Aerospace and Automotive Engineering**:

- Aerodynamic calculations require precise information about the viscosity of air and other gases, which affects drag and heat transfer around moving objects.

4. **Environmental Engineering**:

- Predicting the spread of pollutants in water bodies involves understanding the kinematic viscosity of the water, which affects the dispersion and mixing of contaminants.

Non-Newtonian Systems: A Comprehensive Guide
Introduction to Non-Newtonian Systems

Non-Newtonian systems refer to fluids whose viscosity is not constant and changes with the applied shear rate or shear stress. Unlike Newtonian fluids, these fluids do not follow Newton's law of viscosity. Non-Newtonian behavior is commonly observed in complex fluids such as slurries, pastes, gels, and polymer solutions. Understanding these systems is crucial in various industries, including pharmaceuticals, food processing, cosmetics, and materials science.

Types of Non-Newtonian Fluids

Non-Newtonian fluids can be categorized based on their flow behavior under shear stress. The primary types include pseudoplastic (shear-thinning), dilatant (shear-thickening), plastic, and thixotropic fluids.

1. **Pseudoplastic (Shear-Thinning) Fluids**

   - **Definition**: Pseudoplastic fluids exhibit a decrease in viscosity with an increase in shear rate. This behavior is also known as shear-thinning.
   - **Examples**: Paints, ketchup, blood, and polymer solutions.
   - **Applications**: Shear-thinning behavior is advantageous in applications requiring easy spreading or pumping at high shear rates but high viscosity at rest to prevent settling or dripping.

2. **Dilatant (Shear-Thickening) Fluids**

   - **Definition**: Dilatant fluids exhibit an increase in viscosity with an increase in shear rate. This behavior is also known as shear-thickening.
   - **Examples**: Cornstarch in water (oobleck), certain suspensions and slurries.
   - **Applications**: Shear-thickening materials are used in protective gear, such as body armor, where increased viscosity under impact provides enhanced protection.

3. **Plastic Fluids**

   - **Definition**: Plastic fluids behave like solids under low shear stress and flow like liquids above a certain yield stress.
   - **Subtypes**:

     - **Bingham Plastics**: These have a constant viscosity once the yield stress is exceeded (e.g., toothpaste, mayonnaise).

- **Herschel-Bulkley Fluids**: These have a varying viscosity after exceeding the yield stress.

- **Applications**: Used in products requiring shape retention until a certain stress is applied, such as in construction materials (cement) and food products.

4. Thixotropy

- **Definition**: Thixotropic fluids decrease in viscosity over time when subjected to constant shear stress, and their viscosity recovers when the stress is removed.
- **Examples**: Gelatin, yogurt, certain clays and drilling muds.
- **Applications**: Thixotropy is beneficial in formulations where temporary fluidization is needed, such as in paints that need to flow easily during application but stay in place afterward.

Thixotropy in Formulation

Thixotropy plays a critical role in the formulation of various products, enhancing their performance and user experience:

1. Paints and Coatings:

- Thixotropic paints flow easily when brushed or sprayed, providing smooth application, but regain viscosity quickly to prevent drips and runs.

2. Pharmaceuticals:

- Thixotropic gels and creams are easy to spread but stay in place after application, improving their efficacy and user convenience.

3. **Cosmetics**:

- Products like mascaras and lotions leverage thixotropy for ease of application and enhanced stability.

4. **Food Products**:

- Thixotropic behavior in sauces and dressings ensures they are pourable yet thick enough to adhere to food.

5. **Industrial Applications**:

- In drilling, thixotropic drilling muds help in suspending cuttings and preventing their settlement when circulation stops.

Determination of Viscosity: Methods and Techniques
Introduction to Viscosity Measurement

Viscosity is a fundamental property of fluids that describes their resistance to flow. Accurate determination of viscosity is crucial in various fields such as engineering, pharmaceuticals, food science, and materials research. Several methods are used to measure viscosity, each suited to different types of fluids and conditions. The primary methods include capillary viscometers, falling sphere viscometers, and rotational viscometers.

Capillary Viscometers

Capillary viscometers measure the viscosity of a fluid by observing the time it takes for the fluid to flow through a narrow tube (capillary) under the influence of gravity. The most common types of capillary viscometers are the Ostwald and Ubbelohde viscometers.

1. **Ostwald Viscometer**:

   - **Principle**: The fluid flows through a capillary tube, and the time taken for a set volume of fluid to pass between two marked points is measured.
   - **Equation**: The viscosity ($?\eta$) is calculated using the Hagen-Poiseuille equation: $?=?\cdot?\cdot?\eta=K\cdot\rho\cdot t$ Where $?K$ is a calibration constant, $?\rho$ is the fluid density, and $?t$ is the flow time.
   - **Applications**: Suitable for low to moderately viscous Newtonian fluids such as water, oils, and dilute polymer solutions.

2. **Ubbelohde Viscometer**:

   - **Principle**: Similar to the Ostwald viscometer but designed to minimize errors due to capillary action and hydrostatic pressure.
   - **Advantage**: The Ubbelohde viscometer allows for more precise measurements and is less affected by changes in fluid level.

Falling Sphere Viscometers

Falling sphere viscometers determine viscosity by measuring the terminal velocity of a sphere falling through the fluid. The method is based on Stokes' law, which relates the viscous drag force to the velocity of the sphere.

1. **Principle**:

- A sphere of known size and density is dropped into a fluid.
- The time taken for the sphere to fall a specified distance is recorded.
- The terminal velocity (??*vt*) is used to calculate the viscosity (?*η*) using Stokes' law: ?=2(??–??)??29??*η*=9*vt* 2(*ρs–ρf*)*gr*2 Where ??*ρs* is the density of the sphere, ??*ρf* is the density of the fluid, ?*g* is the acceleration due to gravity, and ?*r* is the radius of the sphere.
- **Applications**: Suitable for both Newtonian and non-Newtonian fluids, particularly for fluids with higher viscosities such as syrups, oils, and polymer melts.

Rotational Viscometers

Rotational viscometers measure viscosity by rotating a spindle or bob within the fluid and measuring the torque required to maintain a constant rotational speed. These instruments can handle a wide range of viscosities and are suitable for both Newtonian and non-Newtonian fluids.

1. **Types of Rotational Viscometers**:

- **Coaxial Cylinder Viscometer** (Couette Flow):

  - **Principle**: A bob rotates within a stationary cup filled with fluid, or the cup rotates around a stationary bob.
  - **Equation**: Viscosity is determined from the torque and rotational speed, often using empirical or

analytical models.

- **Cone and Plate Viscometer**:

  - **Principle**: A cone rotates against a flat plate with a thin layer of fluid between them.
  - **Equation**: Viscosity is calculated from the torque and the angular velocity, taking into account the geometry of the cone and plate.

- **Brookfield Viscometer**:

  - **Principle**: A spindle of various shapes rotates in the fluid, and the torque required to maintain a constant speed is measured.
  - **Applications**: Widely used in industries for quality control of products like paints, coatings, food, and cosmetics.

2. **Advantages**:

- Rotational viscometers can measure a broad range of viscosities.
- They provide detailed information about the rheological properties of non-Newtonian fluids, including shear-thinning, shear-thickening, and viscoelastic behavior.

Deformation of Solids: Plastic and Elastic Deformation

Introduction to Deformation of Solids

Deformation of solids refers to the change in shape or size of a material under an applied force. Understanding the nature of deformation is crucial in fields like materials science, engineering, and structural analysis. Deformation can be broadly classified into two types: elastic deformation and plastic deformation. Each type of deformation has distinct characteristics and occurs under different conditions of stress and strain.

Elastic Deformation

Elastic deformation is a temporary change in the shape or size of a material that is fully reversible upon the removal of the applied load. It follows Hooke's Law, which states that the strain in the material is directly proportional to the applied stress within the elastic limit of that material.

1. **Characteristics**:

   - **Reversibility**: The material returns to its original shape and size after the removal of the force.
   - **Proportionality**: Stress and strain are linearly related within the elastic limit.
   - **Elastic Limit**: The maximum stress that a material can withstand without permanent deformation.

2. **Hooke's Law**:

   - Mathematically expressed as: $?=?\cdot?\sigma=E\cdot\epsilon$ Where:

     - $?\sigma$ is the stress.
     - $?E$ is the Young's modulus of elasticity (a measure of stiffness).
     - $?\epsilon$ is the strain.

3. **Examples**:

- Stretching of a rubber band within its limit.
- Bending of a steel beam under a load that does not exceed its elastic limit.

4. **Applications**:

- Design of springs, elastic bearings, and other components where reversible deformation is desired.
- Structural engineering where materials must return to their original shape after loading, such as bridges and buildings.

Plastic Deformation

Plastic deformation is a permanent change in shape or size of a material that occurs when the material is subjected to stresses beyond its elastic limit. Unlike elastic deformation, plastic deformation is not reversible, and the material retains the deformed shape even after the removal of the applied load.

1. **Characteristics**:

- **Permanence**: The material does not return to its original shape after the force is removed.
- **Yield Point**: The stress level at which a material begins to deform plastically.
- **Non-linear Stress-Strain Relationship**: Beyond the elastic limit, the relationship between stress and strain is no longer linear.

2. **Mechanisms**:

- **Dislocation Movement**: In crystalline materials,

plastic deformation occurs primarily through the movement of dislocations within the crystal lattice.
- **Slip and Twinning**: Specific planes within the crystal structure slide past one another (slip) or mirror image movements form (twinning).

3. **Examples**:

- Bending a paperclip permanently out of shape.
- Metal forming processes such as forging, rolling, and extrusion.

4. **Applications**:

- Metalworking and manufacturing processes that shape materials into desired forms.
- Designing crash structures in automobiles to absorb energy through plastic deformation during an impact.

Comparison of Elastic and Plastic Deformation

1. **Reversibility**:

- **Elastic**: Reversible.
- **Plastic**: Irreversible.

2. **Stress-Strain Relationship**:

- **Elastic**: Linear (Hooke's Law).
- **Plastic**: Non-linear beyond the yield point.

3. **Energy Absorption**:

- **Elastic**: Energy is stored and released.
- **Plastic**: Energy is dissipated through permanent deformation.

4. Behavior Under Load:

- **Elastic**: Deforms and returns to original shape.
- **Plastic**: Deforms and stays deformed.

Understanding the Heckel Equation, Stress, Strain, and Elastic Modulus

Introduction

The mechanical behavior of materials under various forces is a critical aspect of material science and engineering. Key concepts like stress, strain, and elastic modulus help in understanding how materials deform and withstand external loads. Additionally, the Heckel equation provides insights into the densification of powders during compaction, which is particularly relevant in pharmaceutical and materials engineering.

Heckel Equation

The Heckel equation is used to describe the densification of powders under pressure, commonly applied in the pharmaceutical industry to understand the compaction behavior of powders into tablets.

1. Formulation:

- The Heckel equation is expressed as: ln (11−?)=?·?+?ln(1−D1)=K·P+A Where:

  - ?D is the relative density of the powder compact.

- ?*P* is the applied pressure.
- ?*K* and ?*A* are constants specific to the material.

- ?*K* is related to the material's plasticity, indicating how easily it deforms under pressure.
- ?*A* represents the initial porosity of the powder bed.

2. **Applications**:

- Used in the pharmaceutical industry to optimize tablet formulation and manufacturing processes.
- Helps in understanding the compaction behavior and mechanical properties of powder materials.

3. **Interpretation**:

- The slope ?*K* of the linear plot in the Heckel equation indicates the material's ability to undergo plastic deformation.
- A higher ?*K* value suggests a more plastic material, while a lower value indicates a more brittle material.

Stress

Stress is a measure of the internal forces within a material that arise due to externally applied loads. It is defined as the force per unit area and can be categorized into different types depending on the nature of the applied force.

1. **Types of Stress**:

- **Tensile Stress**: Occurs when a material is subjected to a pulling force, leading to elongation.

- **Compressive Stress**: Occurs when a material is subjected to a pushing force, leading to compression.
- **Shear Stress**: Occurs when a material is subjected to forces parallel to its surface, leading to deformation in a plane.

2. **Mathematical Expression**:

- Stress ($?\sigma$) is calculated as: $?=??\sigma=AF$ Where:

  - $?F$ is the applied force.
  - $?A$ is the cross-sectional area over which the force is distributed.

Strain

Strain is a measure of the deformation of a material in response to an applied stress. It is a dimensionless quantity representing the relative change in shape or size.

1. **Types of Strain**:

- **Tensile Strain**: Relative elongation of a material under tensile stress.
- **Compressive Strain**: Relative shortening of a material under compressive stress.
- **Shear Strain**: Change in shape of a material under shear stress.

2. **Mathematical Expression**:

- Strain ($?\epsilon$) is calculated as: $?=\Delta??0\epsilon=L0\Delta L$ Where:

- Δ?ΔL is the change in length.
- ?0$L0$ is the original length.

Elastic Modulus

The **elastic modulus**, also known as the modulus of elasticity, is a measure of a material's stiffness or rigidity. It quantifies the relationship between stress and strain in the elastic deformation region, where the material returns to its original shape upon the removal of the applied load.

1. **Types of Elastic Moduli**:

   - **Young's Modulus (E)**: Measures the stiffness of a material in tension or compression.
   - **Shear Modulus (G)**: Measures the stiffness of a material under shear stress.
   - **Bulk Modulus (K)**: Measures the stiffness of a material under uniform pressure.

2. **Mathematical Expression**:

   - Young's Modulus is given by: ?=??$E=\epsilon\sigma$ Where:

     - ?σ is the tensile stress.
     - ?ϵ is the tensile strain.

3. **Applications**:

   - Determines the mechanical behavior of materials in structural and mechanical engineering.
   - Helps in the design and analysis of load-bearing components and structures.

Coarse Dispersion: An Overview

Introduction to Coarse Dispersions

A coarse dispersion is a type of heterogeneous mixture where one substance (the dispersed phase) is distributed in larger particles within another substance (the continuous phase). These particles are typically larger than 1 micrometer and can be seen with the naked eye or a light microscope. Coarse dispersions are commonly encountered in everyday life and have numerous applications in various industries, including pharmaceuticals, food, cosmetics, and materials science.

Characteristics of Coarse Dispersions

1. **Particle Size**:

   - The dispersed particles in a coarse dispersion range from 1 micrometer to several millimeters.
   - Because of their large size, these particles tend to settle out or separate from the continuous phase over time if left undisturbed.

2. **Visibility**:

   - Particles are often visible to the naked eye or can be easily seen under a light microscope.
   - The dispersions can appear cloudy or turbid due to the scattering of light by the large particles.

3. **Stability**:

   - Coarse dispersions are generally less stable than colloidal dispersions or true solutions.
   - Over time, particles may settle due to gravity,

necessitating mechanical agitation or the use of stabilizing agents to maintain uniformity.

4. **Examples**:

- Common examples include suspensions (solid particles in a liquid), emulsions (liquid droplets in another liquid), and foams (gas bubbles in a liquid or solid).

Types of Coarse Dispersions

1. **Suspensions**:

- A suspension consists of solid particles dispersed in a liquid medium.
- Example: Muddy water, where soil particles are suspended in water.
- Applications: Pharmaceutical suspensions for delivering poorly soluble drugs, paint formulations, and wastewater treatment.

2. **Emulsions**:

- An emulsion is a mixture of two immiscible liquids where one liquid is dispersed as droplets within the other.
- Example: Oil and vinegar in salad dressing.
- Applications: Cosmetics (creams and lotions), food products (mayonnaise and sauces), and pharmaceuticals (emulsified drugs).

3. **Foams**:

- Foams consist of gas bubbles dispersed in a liquid or solid matrix.
- Example: Whipped cream, where air bubbles are trapped in a cream matrix.
- Applications: Food products, insulation materials, and firefighting foams.

Stability and Instability in Coarse Dispersions

1. **Settling and Sedimentation**:

   - Due to gravity, larger particles in a coarse dispersion tend to settle at the bottom over time.
   - Sedimentation rate can be influenced by particle size, density difference between the dispersed and continuous phases, and viscosity of the continuous phase.

2. **Flocculation and Coalescence**:

   - **Flocculation**: Particles aggregate to form flocs or clusters, which can then settle more rapidly.
   - **Coalescence**: Droplets in an emulsion merge to form larger droplets, leading to phase separation.

3. **Stabilization Methods**:

   - **Mechanical Agitation**: Regular stirring or shaking can help maintain the uniformity of the dispersion.
   - **Stabilizing Agents**: Surfactants, thickeners, and emulsifiers can be added to prevent settling and coalescence by increasing the viscosity of the continuous phase or by creating a barrier around the

dispersed particles.

Applications of Coarse Dispersions

1. **Pharmaceuticals**:

   - Suspensions and emulsions are commonly used to deliver drugs that are poorly soluble in water. Ensuring proper dosage and bioavailability is critical in these formulations.

2. **Food Industry**:

   - Many food products are coarse dispersions, such as sauces, dressings, and dairy products. Stabilizers and emulsifiers are often used to maintain texture and consistency.

3. **Cosmetics**:

   - Creams, lotions, and other cosmetic products are often emulsions that require careful formulation to ensure stability and pleasant sensory properties.

4. **Materials Science**:

   - Coarse dispersions are used in the formulation of paints, coatings, and construction materials, where the dispersion of pigments or fillers is crucial for performance and aesthetics.

Understanding Suspensions and Interfacial Properties

Introduction to Suspensions

A suspension is a type of coarse dispersion where solid particles are dispersed within a liquid medium. The particles in a suspension are larger than those in a colloid and can often be seen with the naked eye. Suspensions are a common form of mixture used in various fields, including pharmaceuticals, food, cosmetics, and industrial processes.

Characteristics of Suspensions

1. **Particle Size**:

   - The particles in a suspension are typically larger than 1 micrometer.
   - Because of their size, these particles do not dissolve in the liquid but remain dispersed.

2. **Visibility**:

   - Suspensions often appear cloudy or opaque due to the scattering of light by the dispersed particles.

3. **Stability**:

   - Suspensions are generally unstable over time. Particles tend to settle out due to gravity if the mixture is left undisturbed.

Interfacial Properties of Suspended Particles

The behavior and stability of suspended particles are significantly influenced by their interfacial properties. These properties are critical in determining how particles interact with each other and with the liquid medium.

1. **Surface Area and Surface Energy**:

   - Particles with a high surface area to volume ratio have higher surface energy, which affects their stability and interaction with the medium.
   - High surface energy can lead to agglomeration as particles seek to minimize their energy by coming together.

2. **Zeta Potential**:

   - Zeta potential is the electrical potential at the slipping plane of a particle in a fluid. It is a key indicator of the stability of suspensions.
   - A high zeta potential (either positive or negative) typically indicates strong repulsion between particles, leading to better stability. Conversely, a low zeta potential can result in particle aggregation.

3. **Surface Charge and Electrostatic Interactions**:

   - Particles can acquire a surface charge in a suspension, often due to ionization of surface groups or adsorption of ions from the surrounding medium.
   - Electrostatic repulsion between similarly charged particles can help maintain the stability of the suspension by preventing aggregation.

4. **Steric Stabilization**:

   - In addition to electrostatic interactions, particles can be stabilized by adsorbing polymer layers, which create a physical barrier that prevents particles from

coming too close and aggregating.
- Steric stabilization is particularly effective in non-aqueous suspensions.

Settling in Suspensions

Settling is a common issue in suspensions, influenced by various factors such as particle size, density, and the viscosity of the medium. Understanding the settling behavior is crucial for the effective formulation and stabilization of suspensions.

1. **Stokes' Law**:

   - Stokes' Law describes the settling velocity of spherical particles in a fluid. The law is given by: ?=2?2(??−??)?9?v=9η2r2(ρp−ρf)g Where:

     - ?v is the settling velocity.
     - ?r is the radius of the particle.
     - ??ρp is the density of the particle.
     - ??ρf is the density of the fluid.
     - ?g is the acceleration due to gravity.
     - ?η is the viscosity of the fluid.

   - Stokes' Law indicates that larger and denser particles settle faster than smaller and less dense ones.

2. **Sedimentation and Flocculation**:

   - Over time, particles in a suspension may aggregate into larger clusters, a process known as flocculation, which accelerates settling.

- Sedimentation can be influenced by external factors like temperature and agitation.

3. **Preventing Settling**:

- **Viscosity Modification**: Increasing the viscosity of the liquid medium can reduce the settling rate. Thickeners and gelling agents are often used for this purpose.
- **Particle Size Reduction**: Smaller particles settle more slowly. Techniques such as milling can be used to reduce particle size.
- **Stabilizers**: Electrostatic and steric stabilizers can be added to prevent particle aggregation and maintain dispersion stability.

Applications of Suspensions

1. **Pharmaceuticals**:

- Suspensions are used to deliver insoluble drugs. They offer advantages like improved bioavailability and controlled release.
- Examples include pediatric formulations and certain injectable drugs.

2. **Food Industry**:

- Many food products, such as sauces, gravies, and salad dressings, are suspensions. Stabilizers ensure consistency and prevent separation.

3. **Cosmetics**:

- Cosmetic formulations like sunscreens, lotions, and makeup often rely on suspensions to deliver active ingredients and achieve desired textures.

4. **Industrial Processes**:

- Suspensions are used in processes like painting, ceramics, and wastewater treatment.

Formulation of Flocculated and Deflocculated Suspensions

Introduction

Suspensions, which are dispersions of solid particles in a liquid medium, can be formulated as either flocculated or deflocculated systems. The choice between these two types depends on the desired properties and stability of the suspension. Flocculated suspensions contain particles that aggregate into loosely bound clusters (flocs), whereas deflocculated suspensions contain dispersed particles that remain as individual entities. Understanding the principles and methods of formulating these suspensions is crucial in various fields, including pharmaceuticals, food, and cosmetics.

Flocculated Suspensions

Flocculated suspensions are characterized by the presence of flocs, which are aggregates of particles held together by weak forces. These suspensions are typically easier to resuspend after settling but may exhibit rapid sedimentation.

1. **Characteristics**:

- **Sedimentation**: Particles settle rapidly due to the

formation of larger flocs.

- **Redispersibility**: The sediment is loosely packed and easy to redisperse with gentle shaking.
- **Appearance**: Flocculated suspensions often appear cloudy due to the light scattering by the flocs.

2. **Formulation Principles**:

- **Flocculating Agents**: Additives that promote the aggregation of particles into flocs.

  - **Electrolytes**: Adjusting the ionic strength of the medium to reduce repulsive forces between particles.
  - **Polymers**: High molecular weight compounds that can bridge between particles and form flocs.
  - **Surfactants**: Compounds that adsorb onto particle surfaces and reduce the energy barrier for floc formation.

3. **Steps to Formulate Flocculated Suspensions**:

- **Selection of Dispersing Medium**: Choose a suitable liquid medium for the suspension.
- **Dispersion of Particles**: Disperse the solid particles uniformly in the medium using mechanical agitation or ultrasonic treatment.
- **Addition of Flocculating Agents**: Add the chosen flocculating agents to promote the formation of flocs. The concentration and type of flocculating agent are critical for controlling the degree of flocculation.
- **Optimization**: Adjust the pH, ionic strength, and concentration of additives to achieve the desired

balance between stability and resuspendability.

Deflocculated Suspensions

Deflocculated suspensions are those in which the particles remain as discrete entities and do not form aggregates. These suspensions generally exhibit slower sedimentation but may form a hard, compact sediment that is difficult to resuspend.

1. **Characteristics**:

   - **Sedimentation**: Particles settle slowly, resulting in a more uniform suspension over time.
   - **Redispersibility**: The sediment tends to be more compact and may require vigorous shaking to redisperse.
   - **Appearance**: Deflocculated suspensions often appear more transparent, as particles are individually dispersed.

2. **Formulation Principles**:

   - **Dispersing Agents**: Additives that prevent the aggregation of particles.

     - **Surfactants**: Reduce surface tension and prevent particles from coming together.
     - **Polymers**: Adsorb onto particle surfaces and provide steric stabilization.
     - **pH Adjusters**: Modify the pH to increase the surface charge of particles, enhancing repulsive forces.

3. **Steps to Formulate Deflocculated Suspensions**:

   - **Selection of Dispersing Medium**: Choose a suitable liquid medium for the suspension.
   - **Particle Size Reduction**: Use techniques like milling or homogenization to reduce particle size, which helps in achieving better dispersion.
   - **Addition of Dispersing Agents**: Add surfactants, polymers, or other dispersing agents to maintain particle separation.
   - **Optimization**: Adjust the concentration of dispersing agents, pH, and other formulation parameters to ensure stable deflocculation.

Comparison of Flocculated and Deflocculated Suspensions

1. **Sedimentation Behavior**:

   - **Flocculated**: Rapid sedimentation, forming a loose sediment that is easy to resuspend.
   - **Deflocculated**: Slow sedimentation, forming a compact sediment that may be difficult to resuspend.

2. **Stability**:

   - **Flocculated**: Temporarily stable; requires frequent shaking to maintain uniformity.
   - **Deflocculated**: More stable over time; less frequent agitation needed but harder to redisperse once settled.

3. **Applications**:

- **Flocculated**: Suitable for applications where ease of resuspension is critical, such as in oral suspensions and injectable formulations.
- **Deflocculated**: Suitable for applications requiring long-term stability and uniform dosing, such as topical suspensions and certain industrial applications.

Emulsions: Theories of Emulsification, Microemulsions, and Multiple Emulsions

Introduction to Emulsions

Emulsions are a type of colloidal system where one liquid is dispersed as droplets within another immiscible liquid. Emulsions are commonly used in various industries, including food, pharmaceuticals, cosmetics, and chemical engineering. They can be classified based on the dispersed and continuous phases into oil-in-water (O/W) emulsions, where oil droplets are dispersed in water, and water-in-oil (W/O) emulsions, where water droplets are dispersed in oil.

Theories of Emulsification

Emulsification is the process of creating an emulsion, typically involving the input of energy to disperse one liquid into another immiscible liquid. Several theories explain how emulsification occurs and how emulsions are stabilized.

1. **Surface Tension Theory**:

   - This theory suggests that emulsification occurs by reducing the interfacial tension between the two immiscible liquids.
   - Surfactants or emulsifying agents reduce the surface tension at the oil-water interface, making it easier to

form small droplets.

2. **Surface Film Theory**:

   - According to this theory, surfactants form a monomolecular layer around the dispersed droplets, preventing them from coalescing.
   - This film acts as a mechanical barrier, stabilizing the emulsion by reducing the tendency of the droplets to merge.

3. **Repulsion Theory**:

   - This theory proposes that the electrical charges on the surface of droplets (due to the adsorption of ionic surfactants) create repulsive forces between droplets.
   - These repulsive forces prevent droplets from coming together and coalescing, thereby stabilizing the emulsion.

4. **Viscosity Theory**:

   - Increasing the viscosity of the continuous phase can help stabilize emulsions by slowing down the movement of dispersed droplets.
   - Thickeners and gelling agents are often added to emulsions to increase viscosity and improve stability.

Microemulsions

Microemulsions are clear, thermodynamically stable mixtures of oil, water, and surfactant, often with a co-surfactant. They differ from conventional emulsions in their transparency, stability, and droplet size.

Emulsion stability is a critical aspect of formulating and maintaining emulsions for various applications, including pharmaceuticals, food products, cosmetics, and industrial processes. Stability refers to the ability of an emulsion to resist changes in its properties over time. Unstable emulsions can separate into their constituent phases, leading to product failure and reduced efficacy.

Factors Affecting Emulsion Stability

1. **Droplet Size and Distribution:**

   - Smaller droplet sizes and uniform distribution contribute to higher stability. Smaller droplets reduce the likelihood of coalescence and creaming.

2. **Viscosity of Continuous Phase:**

   - Increasing the viscosity of the continuous phase slows down the movement of droplets, reducing the rate of sedimentation or creaming.

3. **Interfacial Tension:**

   - Lowering interfacial tension between the oil and water phases through the use of surfactants helps stabilize the emulsion by reducing the energy required to form and maintain small droplets.

4. **Electrical Charges and Zeta Potential:**

   - The presence of electrical charges on droplet surfaces (due to ionic surfactants) creates repulsive forces that prevent droplet coalescence, enhancing stability.

5. **Temperature and Storage Conditions**:

   - Temperature fluctuations can lead to changes in viscosity, interfacial tension, and phase separation. Stable emulsions are formulated to withstand these changes.

Types of Emulsion Instability

1. **Creaming**:

   - The upward movement of dispersed droplets to form a cream layer. This is usually reversible upon shaking but indicates partial instability.

2. **Sedimentation**:

   - The downward movement of dispersed droplets. Like creaming, this can often be reversed by shaking but is undesirable in stable emulsions.

3. **Flocculation**:

   - The aggregation of droplets into loose clusters (flocs) without merging. Flocculation can lead to coalescence over time if not controlled.

4. **Coalescence**:

   - The merging of droplets into larger ones, leading to phase separation. This is usually irreversible and signifies a breakdown of the emulsion.

5. **Ostwald Ripening**:

   - The process where smaller droplets dissolve and redeposit onto larger ones, leading to an increase in average droplet size. This is driven by the difference in solubility between small and large droplets.

Methods to Enhance Emulsion Stability

1. **Use of Emulsifiers**:

   - Emulsifiers (surfactants) reduce interfacial tension and form a protective layer around droplets. Common emulsifiers include lecithin, polysorbates, and sodium lauryl sulfate.

2. **Thickeners and Stabilizers**:

   - Adding thickeners like gums (xanthan, guar) and polymers (carbomers, polyvinyl alcohol) increases the viscosity of the continuous phase, reducing droplet mobility.

3. **pH Adjustment**:

   - Adjusting the pH can optimize the charge on droplet surfaces, enhancing electrostatic stabilization. Buffering agents can maintain a stable pH environment.

4. **Temperature Control**:

   - Maintaining a consistent temperature during

formulation and storage prevents changes in viscosity and interfacial tension that can destabilize the emulsion.

5. **Homogenization**:

- High-shear mixing or homogenization techniques can reduce droplet size and create a more uniform droplet distribution, contributing to stability.

Preservation of Emulsions

Preservation is essential to prevent microbial growth and chemical degradation in emulsions, ensuring their safety and efficacy throughout their shelf life.

1. **Antimicrobial Preservatives**:

- Preservatives such as parabens, benzyl alcohol, and phenoxyethanol are added to emulsions to inhibit the growth of bacteria, fungi, and yeasts. The choice of preservative depends on the emulsion's pH, phase compatibility, and regulatory considerations.

2. **Antioxidants**:

- Antioxidants like ascorbic acid (vitamin C), tocopherols (vitamin E), and butylated hydroxytoluene (BHT) are used to prevent oxidation of the oil phase, which can lead to rancidity and degradation of active ingredients.

3. **Chelating Agents**:

- Chelating agents such as ethylenediaminetetraacetic acid (EDTA) bind metal ions that catalyze oxidation reactions, enhancing the stability of the emulsion.

4. **Proper Packaging**:

   - Packaging plays a critical role in preserving emulsions. Containers that protect from light, air, and contamination help maintain stability. Airtight and opaque containers are often used to prevent oxidative degradation and microbial contamination.

5. **Controlled Storage Conditions**:

   - Storing emulsions at recommended temperatures and avoiding exposure to extreme conditions (heat, light, freezing) helps prolong their stability and efficacy.

Rheological Properties of Emulsions
Introduction to Rheology and Emulsions
Rheology is the study of the flow and deformation of matter, focusing on the properties that define how materials respond to applied forces. In the context of emulsions, which are mixtures of two immiscible liquids where one is dispersed in the other, rheological properties are crucial for determining the behavior, stability, and application of the emulsion. These properties influence how emulsions are processed, stored, and used in various applications, including pharmaceuticals, food products, cosmetics, and industrial formulations.

Key Rheological Properties of Emulsions

1. **Viscosity**:

   - **Definition**: Viscosity is a measure of a fluid's resistance to flow. In emulsions, it depends on factors such as droplet size, droplet concentration, and the properties of the continuous phase.
   - **Measurement**: Viscosity can be measured using viscometers or rheometers. The relationship between shear stress and shear rate often characterizes viscosity.
   - **Influence of Droplet Size and Concentration**: Smaller droplet sizes and higher concentrations of the dispersed phase generally increase the viscosity of an emulsion.

2. **Shear Thinning and Shear Thickening**:

   - **Shear Thinning (Pseudoplasticity)**: Emulsions often exhibit shear thinning behavior, where viscosity decreases with increasing shear rate. This property is beneficial in processes requiring easy spreading or pumping, such as in lotions and creams.
   - **Shear Thickening (Dilatancy)**: Some emulsions can show shear thickening behavior, where viscosity increases with increasing shear rate. This is less common but can occur in concentrated systems.

3. **Thixotropy**:

   - **Definition**: Thixotropy is a time-dependent shear thinning property. When an emulsion is sheared, its viscosity decreases, but it recovers its original viscosity after the shear is removed.

- **Applications**: Thixotropic behavior is advantageous in applications requiring ease of application followed by stability, such as in paints and certain food products.

4. **Yield Stress**:

- **Definition**: Yield stress is the minimum stress required to initiate flow in an emulsion. Below this stress, the emulsion behaves as a solid.
- **Significance**: Emulsions with yield stress do not flow under low stress conditions, which is useful for preventing sedimentation and maintaining shape in products like gels and pastes.

Factors Affecting Rheological Properties of Emulsions

1. **Droplet Size and Distribution**:

- Uniform and small droplet sizes generally lead to higher viscosity and more stable emulsions due to increased surface area and interaction between droplets.

2. **Volume Fraction of Dispersed Phase**:

- Higher volume fractions of the dispersed phase increase viscosity and can lead to non-Newtonian behavior, such as shear thinning or thickening.

3. **Emulsifier Type and Concentration**:

- The choice and concentration of emulsifiers

significantly impact the interfacial properties and hence the rheological behavior. Effective emulsifiers stabilize droplets and influence viscosity.

4. **Continuous Phase Viscosity**:

   - The viscosity of the continuous phase (e.g., water, oil) affects the overall rheology of the emulsion. Thicker continuous phases result in higher viscosity emulsions.

5. **Temperature**:

   - Temperature changes can alter the viscosity of both phases, affect interfacial tension, and thus modify the rheological properties. Higher temperatures generally reduce viscosity.

6. **pH and Ionic Strength**:

   - pH and ionic strength can affect the charge and stability of the emulsifier, leading to changes in droplet interaction and overall rheology.

Measuring Rheological Properties

1. **Viscometers**:

   - Simple and widely used instruments for measuring viscosity at a single shear rate or across a range of shear rates.

2. **Rheometers**:

- Advanced instruments that provide detailed information on flow and deformation, capable of measuring shear thinning, shear thickening, thixotropy, and yield stress.

3. **Oscillatory Rheology**:

- A technique where small oscillatory strains are applied to measure the viscoelastic properties of emulsions, providing insights into both the liquid and solid-like behavior.

Practical Implications

1. **Pharmaceuticals**:

- Rheological properties influence the stability, texture, and delivery of pharmaceutical emulsions. Control over these properties ensures effective drug delivery and patient compliance.

2. **Food Products**:

- The mouthfeel, spreadability, and stability of food emulsions (like dressings, sauces, and creams) are dictated by their rheology. Adjusting rheological properties helps achieve desired sensory attributes and shelf life.

3. **Cosmetics**:

- Cosmetic emulsions (like lotions, creams, and sunscreens) rely on rheological properties for ease of application, stability, and aesthetic appeal. Optimizing these properties enhances user experience and product performance.

4. **Industrial Applications**:

- In paints, lubricants, and other industrial products, rheological properties determine application characteristics, stability, and performance under various conditions.

Emulsion Formulation by the HLB Method
Introduction to Emulsions and HLB

Emulsions are mixtures of two immiscible liquids where one is dispersed in the other in the form of small droplets. They are widely used in pharmaceuticals, cosmetics, food products, and various industrial applications. The Hydrophilic-Lipophilic Balance (HLB) method is a systematic approach for selecting the appropriate emulsifiers to stabilize emulsions.

Understanding the HLB System

The HLB system, developed by Griffin in the 1940s, provides a numerical scale to describe the balance between the hydrophilic (water-loving) and lipophilic (oil-loving) parts of a surfactant molecule. The HLB value ranges from 0 to 20:

- **Low HLB Values (0-6)**: Indicate lipophilic (oil-soluble) surfactants, suitable for water-in-oil (W/O) emulsions.
- **High HLB Values (10-20)**: Indicate hydrophilic (water-soluble) surfactants, suitable for oil-in-water (O/W) emulsions.
- **Intermediate HLB Values (7-9)**: Represent surfactants

that can act as wetting agents or detergents.

Steps in Emulsion Formulation by the HLB Method

1. **Determine the Required HLB of the Oil Phase**:

   - Each oil or combination of oils used in the emulsion has a specific HLB requirement for optimal emulsification.
   - The required HLB for a mixture of oils can be calculated by averaging the HLB values of the individual oils, weighted by their proportion in the mixture.

2. **Select Emulsifiers**:

   - Choose surfactants with HLB values close to the required HLB of the oil phase.
   - Often, a combination of surfactants is used to achieve the desired HLB. The overall HLB can be calculated using the weighted average of the HLB values of the selected surfactants.

3. **Calculate the Proportions of Emulsifiers**:

   - Determine the required amounts of each surfactant to achieve the desired HLB value. For example, if two surfactants with HLB values HLB1 and HLB2 are used in proportions X1 and X2 respectively, the overall HLB can be calculated as:

HLBmixture=(?1×???1)+(?2×???2)HLBmixture
$=(X1×HLB1)+(X2×HLB2)$

- Adjust the proportions until the required HLB is met.

4. **Prepare the Emulsion**:

   - Heat the oil and water phases separately to an appropriate temperature (often 70-80°C) to facilitate mixing.
   - Add the emulsifiers to the oil phase or the water phase, depending on their solubility.
   - Slowly combine the oil and water phases while stirring vigorously to form the emulsion.
   - Homogenize the mixture using high-shear mixing or homogenization to achieve the desired droplet size and distribution.

Example of Emulsion Formulation Using HLB Method

Consider formulating an O/W emulsion with the following ingredients:

- **Oil Phase**: Mineral oil and lanolin
- **Water Phase**: Water
- **Emulsifiers**: A blend of Span 80 (HLB = 4.3) and Tween 80 (HLB = 15)

1. **Calculate the Required HLB**:

   - Suppose the required HLB for mineral oil is 10.5 and for lanolin is 8.5.
   - If the oil phase consists of 70% mineral oil and 30% lanolin, the required HLB is:

Required HLB=(0.7×10.5)+(0.3×8.5)=9.9Required HLB=(0.7×10.5)+(0.3×8.5)=9.9

2. **Select and Combine Emulsifiers**:

- Choose Span 80 (HLB = 4.3) and Tween 80 (HLB = 15) to achieve an HLB of 9.9.
- Calculate the proportions of Span 80 (X1) and Tween 80 (X2) required:

9.9=(?1×4.3)+(?2×15)9.9=(X1×4.3)+(X2×15)

Since ?1+?2=1X1+X2=1, solve the equations simultaneously:

9.9=(?1×4.3)+((1−?1)×15)9.9=(X1×4.3)+((1−X1)×15)
9.9=4.3?1+15−15?19.9=4.3X1+15−15X1
9.9=15−10.7?19.9=15−10.7X1
10.7?1=15−9.910.7X1=15−9.9
?1=5.110.7≈0.476X1=10.75.1≈0.476
?2=1−0.476=0.524X2=1−0.476=0.524

- Use 47.6% Span 80 and 52.4% Tween 80 in the emulsifier blend.

3. **Prepare the Emulsion**:

- Heat the oil phase (containing mineral oil, lanolin, and emulsifiers) and the water phase separately.
- Combine the phases while stirring vigorously.
- Homogenize the emulsion to achieve a fine and stable dispersion.

Benefits of Using the HLB Method

- **Systematic Approach**: Provides a rational and systematic way to select emulsifiers based on the specific requirements of the oil phase.
- **Predictable Outcomes**: Enhances the likelihood of forming stable emulsions with desired properties.
- **Flexibility**: Allows the use of combinations of emulsifiers to tailor the HLB value precisely.

Limitations of the HLB Method

- **Simplification**: The method simplifies the complex interactions in emulsions and may not account for all factors affecting stability.
- **Empirical Nature**: Requires empirical adjustments and testing to fine-tune the formulation.
- **Limited Scope**: Primarily applicable to non-ionic surfactants and may not be as effective for ionic surfactants or complex emulsions.

Micromeritics: The Science of Small Particles
Introduction to Micromeritics

Micromeritics is the science and technology of small particles, focusing on the characterization, measurement, and manipulation of particles in the micrometer and nanometer size ranges. This field is crucial in various industries, including pharmaceuticals, materials science, ceramics, and agriculture, where the properties of small particles can significantly impact the performance and quality of products.

Key Concepts in Micromeritics

1. **Particle Size and Size Distribution**:

- **Particle Size**: Refers to the dimensions of individual particles. It is often measured in micrometers (μm) or nanometers (nm).
- **Size Distribution**: Describes the range and frequency of particle sizes in a sample. Understanding size distribution helps predict how particles will behave in a mixture or formulation.

2. **Particle Shape**:

- Particles can be spherical, cylindrical, irregular, or have other shapes. The shape affects properties like flowability, packing, and surface area.

3. **Surface Area**:

- The total surface area of particles per unit mass or volume. It is critical for reactions, dissolution rates, and adsorption processes. Higher surface area often means more reactive or dissolvable particles.

4. **Porosity and Pore Size Distribution**:

- Porosity is the measure of void spaces within particles. Pore size distribution affects properties such as fluid permeability and mechanical strength.

5. **Density**:

- **Bulk Density**: The mass of particles divided by the total volume they occupy, including voids between particles.
- **True Density**: The mass of particles divided by the

volume of the particles themselves, excluding voids.

6. **Flow Properties**:

- Describes how particles move and interact under different conditions. Important for processes like mixing, transport, and compaction.

Methods of Particle Characterization

1. **Laser Diffraction**:

- Measures particle size distribution by analyzing the pattern of light scattered by particles. Suitable for a wide range of sizes and used in various industries.

2. **Dynamic Light Scattering (DLS)**:

- Measures the size of small particles and molecules in suspension or solution by analyzing fluctuations in scattered light.

3. **Sieving**:

- A traditional method where particles are passed through a series of sieves with different mesh sizes to determine size distribution.

4. **Electron Microscopy**:

- Provides detailed images of particle shape and surface features. Scanning Electron Microscopy (SEM) and Transmission Electron Microscopy (TEM) are commonly used techniques.

5. **Gas Adsorption (BET Analysis)**:

   - Measures surface area and porosity by analyzing the amount of gas adsorbed onto the particle surface at different pressures.

6. **Mercury Intrusion Porosimetry**:

   - Measures pore size distribution and porosity by analyzing the pressure required to force mercury into the pores of a sample.

7. **Sedimentation Techniques**:

   - Measure particle size distribution based on the rate of sedimentation of particles in a fluid. Stokes' law is often applied to relate sedimentation rate to particle size.

Importance of Micromeritics in Various Industries

1. **Pharmaceuticals**:

   - **Drug Formulation**: Particle size affects drug solubility, dissolution rate, and bioavailability. Micromeritics helps in designing effective and stable formulations.
   - **Quality Control**: Ensures consistency and efficacy of pharmaceutical products by controlling particle properties.

2. **Materials Science**:

   - **Composite Materials**: Particle size and distribution influence the mechanical properties and performance of composites.
   - **Catalysts**: High surface area particles enhance the activity and efficiency of catalysts.

3. **Cosmetics**:

   - **Texture and Feel**: Particle size affects the texture, feel, and application properties of cosmetic products.
   - **Stability**: Helps in formulating stable and homogenous products.

4. **Food Industry**:

   - **Texture and Stability**: Particle size influences the texture, stability, and sensory properties of food products.
   - **Processing**: Affects mixing, drying, and packaging processes.

5. **Ceramics and Construction**:

   - **Strength and Durability**: Particle size and distribution impact the mechanical strength and durability of ceramics and construction materials.
   - **Processing**: Affects the ease of mixing, molding, and sintering processes.

Challenges and Future Directions

1. **Nanoparticle Characterization**:

   - As industries move towards the use of nanoparticles, new techniques and methodologies are needed to accurately characterize these extremely small particles.

2. **In-line and Real-time Measurement**:

   - Developing technologies for real-time monitoring of particle properties during manufacturing processes can improve efficiency and product quality.

3. **Sustainable Practices**:

   - Understanding particle properties can lead to more efficient use of materials and energy, contributing to sustainability goals.

4. **Advanced Materials**:

   - Micromeritics is crucial for the development of advanced materials with tailored properties for specific applications, such as drug delivery systems and high-performance composites.

Particle Size and Distribution: Mean Particle Size Introduction

Particle size and distribution are critical parameters in many fields, including pharmaceuticals, materials science, food technology, and environmental science. These properties significantly influence the behavior and characteristics of particulate materials, affecting processes like mixing, compaction, dissolution, and reaction rates. Understanding particle size and distribution is essential for optimizing product performance and ensuring consistency.

Particle Size

Particle size refers to the dimensions of individual particles in a material. It can be described by various measures, such as diameter for spherical particles or equivalent diameter for irregularly shaped particles. Common methods for defining particle size include:

1. **Sieve Diameter**: The size of particles that pass through a mesh sieve.
2. **Stokes Diameter**: The diameter of a sphere that settles at the same rate as the particle in a fluid.
3. **Volume-Equivalent Diameter**: The diameter of a sphere having the same volume as the particle.

Particle Size Distribution

Particle size distribution describes the range and frequency of particle sizes within a sample. It is typically represented graphically or statistically, providing insight into the proportion of different sized particles present.

1. **Graphical Representations**:

   - **Histograms**: Show the frequency of particles within specific size ranges.
   - **Cumulative Distribution Curves**: Indicate the percentage of particles smaller than a given size.
   - **Log-Normal Plots**: Often used for particle size distributions that follow a log-normal distribution, showing a straight line when plotted on a logarithmic scale.

2. **Statistical Measures**:

- **Median Diameter (D50)**: The size at which 50% of the particles are smaller and 50% are larger.
- **Mode**: The most frequently occurring particle size.
- **Mean Particle Size**: The average size of particles, calculated by various methods.

Mean Particle Size

Mean particle size is a critical parameter that provides a single value representing the central tendency of a particle size distribution. There are several ways to calculate the mean particle size, depending on the application and the distribution's characteristics.

1. **Arithmetic Mean Diameter (D1,0)**:

- Calculated as the simple average of all particle sizes.
-

$$D\_{1,0} = \frac{1}{N} \sum\_{i=1}^{N} d\_i \,]$$ where ?N is the total number of particles, and ??di is the diameter of the ?i-th particle.

2. **Volume Mean Diameter (D4,3)**:

- Weighted by the volume of the particles, emphasizing larger particles.
-

$$D\_{4,3} = \frac{\sum\_{i=1}^{N} d\_i^4}{\sum\_{i=1}^{N} d\_i^3} \,]$$

3. **Surface Area Mean Diameter (D3,2):**

   - Weighted by the surface area, emphasizing smaller particles.
   -

$$D\_\{3,2\} = \frac\{\sum\_\{i=1\}^\{N\} d\_i^3\}\{\sum\_\{i=1\}^\{N\} d\_i^2\}]$$

4. **Harmonic Mean Diameter:**

   - Useful for representing particles in fluid dynamics and other applications.
   -

$$D\_H = \frac\{N\}\{\sum\_\{i=1\}^\{N\} \frac\{1\}\{d\_i\}\}]$$

Importance of Particle Size and Distribution

1. **Pharmaceuticals:**

   - **Dissolution Rate:** Smaller particles dissolve faster, influencing the bioavailability of drugs.
   - **Content Uniformity:** Uniform particle size ensures consistent dosing and efficacy.

2. **Materials Science:**

   - **Mechanical Properties:** Particle size affects the strength, toughness, and elasticity of composite materials.
   - **Sintering Behavior:** In ceramics and metallurgy, particle size influences the sintering process and final product density.

3. Food Technology:

- **Texture and Stability**: Particle size impacts the texture, mouthfeel, and stability of food products like emulsions and suspensions.
- **Processing Efficiency**: Milling, mixing, and drying processes are affected by particle size.

4. Environmental Science:

- **Air and Water Quality**: Particle size distribution helps in understanding pollutant behavior and designing filtration systems.
- **Soil Properties**: Affects water retention, nutrient availability, and soil structure.

Measurement Techniques

1. Sieving:

- Suitable for larger particles (over 45 μm). Involves passing particles through a series of sieves with decreasing mesh sizes.

2. Laser Diffraction:

- Measures particle size distribution by analyzing the pattern of light scattered by a particle ensemble. Suitable for a wide range of sizes (from nanometers to millimeters).

3. Dynamic Light Scattering (DLS):

- Measures the size of small particles in suspension by analyzing fluctuations in scattered light. Best for particles in the nanometer to sub-micrometer range.

4. **Microscopy**:

   - Provides direct visualization of particle size and shape. Techniques include optical microscopy, scanning electron microscopy (SEM), and transmission electron microscopy (TEM).

5. **Sedimentation Methods**:

   - Determine particle size based on the rate of sedimentation in a fluid. Stokes' law is applied to relate sedimentation rate to particle size.

6. **Coulter Counter**:

   - Measures particle size and count by detecting changes in electrical resistance as particles pass through a small orifice.

Particle Size Distribution: Methods and Analysis
Introduction
Particle size distribution is a fundamental characteristic of particulate materials, influencing their behavior and properties in various applications. Understanding the distribution, particle number, and methods for determining particle size is crucial in fields such as pharmaceuticals, materials science, and environmental engineering. This content covers different methods for particle size determination, counting and

separation techniques, and the importance of particle shape.

Particle Size Distribution

Particle size distribution describes the range and frequency of particle sizes within a sample. It provides insight into the proportion of different sized particles and is essential for predicting the material's behavior in processes such as mixing, compaction, dissolution, and reaction rates.

Particle Number

Particle number refers to the total count of particles within a given sample. It is crucial for applications where the number of particles, rather than their mass or volume, determines the material's properties, such as in drug delivery systems, aerosols, and colloidal suspensions.

Methods for Determining Particle Size

Several methods are used to determine particle size and distribution, each with its advantages and limitations. These methods can be broadly classified into counting, separation, and characterization techniques.

1. **Counting Methods:**

   - **Optical Microscopy:**

     - Provides direct visualization and measurement of particle size and shape.
     - Suitable for particles in the micrometer range.
     - Involves counting and measuring particles using image analysis software.

   - **Electron Microscopy:**

     - Includes Scanning Electron Microscopy (SEM)

and Transmission Electron Microscopy (TEM).

- Offers high-resolution images for nanometer-sized particles.
- Used for detailed shape and surface characterization.

- **Coulter Counter**:

    - Measures particle size and count by detecting changes in electrical resistance as particles pass through a small orifice.
    - Suitable for particles ranging from micrometers to a few millimeters.

2. **Separation Methods**:

- **Sieving**:

    - A traditional method for separating particles based on size.
    - Involves passing particles through a series of sieves with decreasing mesh sizes.
    - Suitable for larger particles (over 45 μm).

- **Sedimentation Techniques**:

    - Determines particle size based on the rate of sedimentation in a fluid.
    - Stokes' law relates sedimentation rate to particle size.
    - Includes techniques like the Andreasen pipette and hydrometer analysis.

3. **Characterization Methods**:

- **Laser Diffraction**:

  - Measures particle size distribution by analyzing the pattern of light scattered by a particle ensemble.
  - Suitable for a wide range of sizes (from nanometers to millimeters).
  - Provides rapid and reliable results.

- **Dynamic Light Scattering (DLS)**:

  - Measures the size of small particles in suspension by analyzing fluctuations in scattered light.
  - Best for particles in the nanometer to sub-micrometer range.
  - Commonly used in colloidal and nanoparticle analysis.

- **Gas Adsorption (BET Analysis)**:

  - Measures surface area and porosity by analyzing the amount of gas adsorbed onto the particle surface at different pressures.
  - Used to infer particle size for porous materials.

- **X-ray Diffraction (XRD)**:

  - Used for determining crystallite size in nanomaterials.
  - Analyzes the broadening of X-ray diffraction peaks.

- **Atomic Force Microscopy (AFM):**

  - Provides topographical imaging and size measurement at the nanometer scale.
  - Used for detailed surface characterization.

Particle Shape

Particle shape significantly affects the properties and behavior of particulate materials. Shape descriptors include:

- **Sphericity**: The degree to which a particle approximates a sphere.
- **Aspect Ratio**: The ratio of the longest dimension to the shortest dimension.
- **Surface Roughness**: The texture of the particle surface.

Importance of Particle Shape

1. **Flowability**:

   - Spherical particles generally flow better than irregularly shaped particles.
   - Important for processes such as powder mixing and tablet compression.

2. **Packing Density**:

   - Particle shape influences how particles pack together, affecting bulk density and porosity.
   - Crucial in construction materials and ceramics.

3. **Surface Area**:

- Irregularly shaped particles have a higher surface area than spherical particles of the same volume.
- Affects dissolution rates, catalytic activity, and reaction kinetics.

4. **Mechanical Properties**:

- Shape impacts the strength and durability of composite materials.
- Fibrous or plate-like particles can enhance mechanical reinforcement.

Methods for Determining Particle Shape

1. **Optical Microscopy**:

- Direct observation and measurement of particle shape.
- Image analysis software can quantify shape descriptors.

2. **Electron Microscopy**:

- High-resolution imaging of particle shape and surface features.
- Provides detailed morphological analysis.

3. **Atomic Force Microscopy (AFM)**:

- Topographical imaging at the nanometer scale.
- Used for precise shape and surface characterization.

4. **Laser Diffraction**:

- Can provide some shape information based on the pattern of scattered light.
- Not as detailed as microscopy methods but useful for large samples.

5. **Dynamic Image Analysis**:

- Captures images of particles in motion and analyzes shape descriptors in real-time.
- Suitable for powders and suspensions

Specific Surface Area: Methods for Determining Surface Area

Introduction

Specific surface area (SSA) is a critical parameter in various industries, including pharmaceuticals, materials science, catalysis, and environmental science. It refers to the total surface area of a material per unit of mass, volume, or another specified property. Understanding and accurately measuring the specific surface area is essential for optimizing processes and product performance.

Specific Surface Area

Specific Surface Area (SSA) is defined as the total surface area of a material divided by its mass, volume, or another characteristic measure. It is usually expressed in units of square meters per gram (m^2/g) for powders or square meters per cubic meter (m^2/m^3) for bulk materials. SSA is a critical factor in processes like adsorption, catalysis, dissolution, and reaction kinetics.

Importance of Specific Surface Area

1. **Pharmaceuticals**:

- Influences drug dissolution rates and bioavailability.
- Affects the stability and reactivity of drug formulations.

2. **Catalysis**:

- Higher SSA typically enhances catalytic activity due to increased available active sites.

3. **Materials Science**:

- Impacts mechanical properties and sintering behavior of ceramics and metals.
- Affects the performance of composites and coatings.

4. **Environmental Science**:

- Crucial for adsorption processes in water and air purification.
- Important for understanding soil and sediment properties.

Methods for Determining Surface Area

Several methods are available for measuring the surface area of materials, each with its own advantages and limitations. The choice of method depends on the material type, required precision, and specific application.

1. **Gas Adsorption Methods**:

- **Brunauer-Emmett-Teller (BET) Method**:

  - The most widely used technique for measuring

SSA.

- Based on the physical adsorption of gas molecules (usually nitrogen) onto the surface of the material.
- Provides information on both surface area and pore size distribution.
- The BET equation is applied to the adsorption isotherm to calculate the SSA:

$$1(?0/?-1)=?-1???\cdot??0+1???v(P0/P-1)1=vmcc-1\cdot P0P+vmc1$$

where $?v$ is the volume of gas adsorbed, $?P$ is the pressure, $?0P0$ is the saturation pressure, $??vm$ is the volume of gas required to form a monolayer, and $?c$ is the BET constant.

- **Langmuir Adsorption**:

  - Assumes monolayer adsorption on a homogeneous surface.
  - Less commonly used than BET but applicable for some materials.

2. **Mercury Intrusion Porosimetry**:

- Measures surface area and porosity by analyzing the pressure required to force mercury into the pores of a material.
- Useful for characterizing porous materials, especially those with larger pores.

3. **Microscopy Methods**:

- **Scanning Electron Microscopy (SEM) and Transmission Electron Microscopy (TEM)**:

- Provide detailed images of surface morphology.
- Can be used to estimate surface area, but not as precise as adsorption methods.
- Useful for understanding surface features and roughness.

4. **Dynamic Light Scattering (DLS)**:

  - Measures particle size distribution in suspensions.
  - Can be used to infer surface area if particle shape and density are known.

5. **Atomic Force Microscopy (AFM)**:

  - Provides topographical imaging and surface characterization at the nanometer scale.
  - Useful for detailed surface analysis and roughness measurement.

6. **Gas Permeability**:

  - Measures the flow of gas through a packed bed of particles.
  - Used to infer surface area based on the resistance to gas flow.

7. **Chemical Methods**:

  - **Titration and Reactivity**:

    - Involves reacting the material with a chemical reagent.
    - The extent of reaction is used to estimate surface

area.
- Suitable for materials with specific reactive sites.

Comparison of Methods

- **BET Method**:

  - Widely accepted and versatile.
  - Suitable for a broad range of materials.
  - Provides detailed surface area and pore size information.

- **Mercury Intrusion Porosimetry**:

  - Best for materials with larger pores.
  - Provides both surface area and porosity data.
  - Involves high pressure and toxic mercury, requiring careful handling.

- **Microscopy Methods**:

  - Provide visual and morphological information.
  - Less quantitative for surface area measurement.
  - Essential for understanding surface features.

- **DLS and AFM**:

  - Offer complementary information on particle size and surface characteristics.
  - Not primary methods for SSA measurement but useful for detailed analysis.

Permeability, Adsorption, and Derived Properties of Powders

Introduction

Powders are ubiquitous in various industries, from pharmaceuticals to materials science and food technology. Understanding their properties is crucial for optimizing processes and product performance. This content explores three critical aspects: permeability, adsorption, and derived properties of powders.

Permeability

Permeability refers to the ability of a material to allow fluids (liquids or gases) to pass through it. In the context of powders, permeability is a measure of how easily a fluid can flow through a packed bed of particles.

1. **Factors Affecting Permeability**:

   - **Particle Size and Distribution**: Smaller particles and a broader size distribution typically reduce permeability due to tighter packing and reduced pore spaces.
   - **Particle Shape**: Irregularly shaped particles create more resistance to flow compared to spherical particles.
   - **Porosity**: Higher porosity (more void spaces) generally increases permeability.
   - **Packing Density**: Tightly packed particles reduce permeability.

2. **Measurement of Permeability**:

   - **Darcy's Law**: Used to describe the flow of a fluid through a porous medium.

$?=??\Delta ???Q=\mu LkA\Delta P$

where $?Q$ is the volumetric flow rate, $?k$ is the permeability coefficient, $?A$ is the cross-sectional area, $\Delta ?\Delta P$ is the pressure difference, $?\mu$ is the fluid viscosity, and $?L$ is the length of the medium.

- **Permeameters**: Instruments designed to measure the permeability of powders. Fluid is forced through a sample, and the flow rate and pressure drop are measured to calculate permeability.

3. **Applications**:

- **Filtration**: Designing filters with appropriate permeability to achieve desired flow rates and separation efficiency.
- **Catalysis**: Ensuring adequate flow of reactants through catalyst beds.
- **Pharmaceuticals**: Optimizing tablet formulation and dissolution rates.

Adsorption

Adsorption is the process by which atoms, ions, or molecules from a substance (gas, liquid, or dissolved solid) adhere to a surface. In powders, adsorption occurs on the surface of the particles.

1. **Types of Adsorption**:

- **Physisorption**: Involves weak van der Waals forces. It is reversible and occurs at low temperatures.
- **Chemisorption**: Involves strong chemical bonds. It is usually irreversible and occurs at higher

temperatures.

2. **Factors Affecting Adsorption**:

- **Surface Area**: Higher surface area increases adsorption capacity.
- **Porosity**: Microporous materials with high internal surface areas are particularly effective adsorbents.
- **Surface Chemistry**: Functional groups on the surface can enhance or inhibit adsorption.

3. **Measurement of Adsorption**:

- **BET Method (Brunauer-Emmett-Teller)**: Measures the surface area by nitrogen adsorption.
- **Isotherms**: Adsorption isotherms plot the amount of adsorbate on the adsorbent as a function of its concentration at constant temperature. Common models include Langmuir and Freundlich isotherms.

4. **Applications**:

- **Catalysis**: Catalyst performance is often linked to the adsorption properties.
- **Separation Processes**: Adsorbents are used in gas and liquid phase separations, such as activated carbon for air purification.
- **Pharmaceuticals**: Drug delivery systems utilize adsorption for controlled release.

Derived Properties of Powders

Derived properties of powders are secondary characteristics that arise from primary properties like particle size, shape, and surface area. These include flowability, compressibility, and bulk density.

1. **Flowability**:

   - **Definition**: The ability of a powder to flow under specified conditions.
   - **Factors**: Influenced by particle size, shape, distribution, and moisture content.
   - **Measurement**: Techniques include the angle of repose, flow through an orifice, and shear cell testing.

2. **Compressibility**:

   - **Definition**: The ability of a powder to decrease in volume under pressure.
   - **Factors**: Affected by particle size, shape, and distribution, as well as interparticle forces.
   - **Measurement**: The Carr's Compressibility Index and Hausner ratio are commonly used metrics.

     - **Carr's Index**:

     Carr's Index=(????????????–??????????)????????????×100Carr's Index=$TappedDensity(TappedDensity-BulkDensity)×100$

     - **Hausner Ratio**:

     Hausner Ratio=Tapped DensityBulk DensityHausner Ratio=Bulk DensityTapped Density

3. **Bulk Density**:

- **Definition**: The mass of powder per unit volume, including the void spaces between particles.
- **Factors**: Affected by particle size, shape, and distribution, as well as packing arrangement.
- **Measurement**: Bulk density is measured by filling a container of known volume and weighing the contents. Tapped density is measured after mechanically tapping the container to minimize the volume.

4. **Porosity**:

- **Definition**: The volume fraction of void spaces within a powder bed.

Densities, Bulkiness & Flow Properties of Powders
Introduction

Powders play a crucial role in numerous industries, including pharmaceuticals, food processing, materials science, and cosmetics. Understanding their characteristics, such as porosity, packing arrangement, densities, bulkiness, and flow properties, is essential for optimizing production processes and ensuring the quality and performance of the final products. This content explores these fundamental aspects of powders.

Porosity

Porosity refers to the fraction of the volume of voids (or pores) in a material to the total volume. It is a critical parameter for understanding the behavior of powders in various applications.

1. **Definition and Calculation**:

- **Porosity (??):**

?=?voids?total=?total−?solids?totalϵ=VtotalVvoids =VtotalVtotal−Vsolids

- **Total Porosity** includes all the void spaces, while **effective porosity** considers only the interconnected voids that contribute to fluid flow.

2. **Importance:**

- **Filtration:** High porosity improves filtration efficiency.
- **Catalysis:** Increased surface area available for reactions.
- **Pharmaceuticals:** Affects dissolution rates and bioavailability.

3. **Measurement:**

- **Mercury Intrusion Porosimetry:** Measures the volume of mercury intruded into pores under pressure.
- **Gas Adsorption:** Uses gas adsorption isotherms to determine porosity.

Packing Arrangement

Packing Arrangement refers to how particles are arranged in a powder bed. This arrangement influences the powder's density, porosity, and flow properties.

1. **Types of Packing:**

- **Random Packing**: Particles are randomly arranged, leading to higher porosity.
- **Ordered Packing**: Particles are systematically arranged, resulting in lower porosity and higher packing density. Examples include:

  - **Cubic Packing**: Particles are aligned in a cubic lattice.
  - **Hexagonal Close Packing (HCP)**: Particles are packed as closely as possible in a hexagonal arrangement.

2. **Packing Density**:

   - **Loose Packing**: Achieved when particles settle under gravity alone.
   - **Tapped Density**: Achieved by mechanically tapping or vibrating the container to minimize the volume.

3. **Measurement**:

   - **Bulk Density**: Measured by filling a container with the powder and weighing it.
   - **Tapped Density**: Measured after tapping the container to compact the powder.

Densities

Density of powders can be described in several ways, each providing different insights into the material's characteristics.

1. **True Density**:

- **Definition**: The density of the solid material itself, excluding any voids or pores.
- **Measurement**: Determined using techniques such as helium pycnometry, which measures the volume of gas displaced by the powder.

2. **Bulk Density**:

- **Definition**: The mass of powder per unit volume, including the void spaces between particles.
- **Measurement**: Measured by filling a container of known volume and weighing the contents.

3. **Tapped Density**:

- **Definition**: The density of a powder after it has been compacted by tapping or vibrating.
- **Measurement**: Similar to bulk density but after mechanical tapping to reduce volume.

4. **Importance**:

- **Formulation and Compaction**: Critical for tablet and capsule manufacturing in the pharmaceutical industry.
- **Packaging**: Influences the packaging and transportation efficiency of powdered goods.

Bulkiness

Bulkiness is the inverse of bulk density and provides insight into the volume a given mass of powder occupies.

1. **Definition**:

- **Bulkiness**:

Bulkiness=1Bulk DensityBulkiness=Bulk Density1

2. **Importance**:

- **Handling and Storage**: High bulkiness indicates more volume required for storage.
- **Flow Properties**: Bulkier powders might flow differently compared to denser powders.

Flow Properties

Flow Properties of powders determine how easily they move or flow, which is vital for processes like mixing, conveying, and packing.

1. **Factors Influencing Flow Properties**:

- **Particle Size and Shape**: Smaller and more irregular particles tend to have poorer flow.
- **Moisture Content**: Moisture can lead to clumping and reduced flow.
- **Surface Texture**: Smooth particles generally flow better than rough particles.

2. **Measurement**:

- **Angle of Repose**: The steepest angle at which a pile of powder remains stable.
- **Flow Rate through an Orifice**: Measures the time it takes for a given quantity of powder to pass through a funnel.
- **Shear Cell Testing**: Measures the powder's resistance

to flow under different conditions.

3. **Improving Flow Properties**:

   - **Granulation**: Aggregating finer particles into larger granules.
   - **Additives**: Using flow aids like silica or magnesium stearate.

Drug Stability

Drug stability is a critical aspect of pharmaceutical development and manufacturing, ensuring that medications remain safe, effective, and suitable for use throughout their shelf life. Stability encompasses various factors, including chemical, physical, and microbiological properties of drugs, and is influenced by storage conditions, formulation, packaging, and handling. This content explores the key aspects of drug stability and strategies to maintain it.

Importance of Drug Stability

1. **Safety**: Stable drugs ensure patient safety by maintaining their intended pharmacological properties without degradation or the formation of harmful by-products.
2. **Efficacy**: Stability ensures that drugs retain their therapeutic effectiveness, delivering the desired clinical outcomes over time.
3. **Regulatory Compliance**: Regulatory authorities require pharmaceutical companies to demonstrate drug stability through rigorous testing and documentation to obtain and maintain marketing approval.
4. **Economic Considerations**: Maintaining drug stability

reduces product wastage, minimizes the need for recalls, and supports cost-effective manufacturing and distribution.

Factors Affecting Drug Stability

1. **Chemical Degradation**: Drugs can undergo chemical reactions, such as hydrolysis, oxidation, and photolysis, leading to the formation of degradation products that may be inactive or toxic.
2. **Physical Changes**: Physical instability includes phenomena like polymorphic transitions, crystallization, and changes in particle size or surface area, which can affect drug dissolution rates and bioavailability.
3. **Environmental Factors**: Temperature, humidity, light exposure, and pH can significantly impact drug stability. Environmental stressors can accelerate degradation reactions and reduce shelf life.
4. **Formulation Factors**: Excipients, preservatives, and other formulation components can influence drug stability. Formulation optimization is essential to minimize degradation pathways.

Strategies for Maintaining Drug Stability

1. **Formulation Design**: Selecting excipients and packaging materials that provide protection against degradation and maintain drug stability throughout storage and use.
2. **Container Closure Systems**: Using appropriate packaging, such as amber-colored glass vials or blister packs, to shield drugs from light exposure and prevent

moisture ingress.

3. **Storage Conditions**: Storing drugs under controlled conditions, including temperature and humidity, to minimize degradation. Refrigeration or desiccation may be necessary for certain drugs.

4. **Analytical Testing**: Conducting stability studies under accelerated and long-term storage conditions to monitor degradation kinetics and identify degradation pathways.

5. **Packaging Integrity Testing**: Ensuring the integrity of packaging materials to prevent moisture permeation, oxidation, and other environmental stressors.

6. **Good Manufacturing Practices (GMP)**: Implementing GMP standards to maintain quality control throughout the manufacturing process, including raw material sourcing, production, and packaging.

7. **Stability Indicating Assays**: Developing analytical methods capable of detecting and quantifying degradation products, ensuring accurate assessment of drug stability.

Regulatory Requirements

Regulatory agencies, such as the FDA (U.S. Food and Drug Administration) and EMA (European Medicines Agency), mandate stability testing as part of the drug development process. Guidelines specify the duration, storage conditions, and testing parameters for stability studies, ensuring compliance with regulatory standards.

Reaction Kinetics

Reaction kinetics is the study of the rates at which chemical reactions occur and the factors that influence these rates. It plays a crucial role in various scientific disciplines, including chemistry, biochemistry, chemical engineering, and pharmacology. This content explores the fundamental concepts of reaction kinetics, including rate laws, reaction mechanisms, and factors affecting reaction rates.

Importance of Reaction Kinetics

1. **Understanding Reaction Rates**: Reaction kinetics provides insights into how quickly reactants are consumed and products are formed, essential for predicting reaction outcomes and designing efficient processes.
2. **Optimizing Reaction Conditions**: By studying reaction kinetics, scientists can identify optimal reaction conditions, such as temperature, pressure, and catalysts, to maximize reaction rates and yields.
3. **Designing Chemical Processes**: Reaction kinetics informs the design and optimization of chemical processes in various industries, including pharmaceuticals, petrochemicals, and materials science.
4. **Drug Development**: In pharmacology, reaction kinetics helps assess the rates of drug metabolism, absorption, and elimination, crucial for understanding drug efficacy and toxicity.

Rate Laws

Rate laws describe the relationship between the rate of a chemical reaction and the concentrations of reactants. They are determined experimentally and provide valuable information about the reaction mechanism.

1. **General Form**: The rate law for a generic reaction $aA+bB \rightarrow cC+dD$ is expressed as:

$$\text{Rate} = [?]?[?]?\text{Rate} = k[A]m[B]n$$

where $?k$ is the rate constant, $[?][A]$ and $[?][B]$ are the concentrations of reactants A and B, respectively, and $?m$ and $?n$ are the reaction orders with respect to A and B, respectively.

2. **Order of Reaction**: The sum of the reaction orders with respect to each reactant determines the overall order of the reaction.
3. **Rate Constant**: The rate constant $?k$ is specific to each reaction and depends on temperature, pressure, and catalysts.

Reaction Mechanisms

Reaction mechanisms describe the sequence of elementary steps by which a chemical reaction occurs. Complex reactions often involve multiple elementary steps, and understanding the mechanism provides insights into the reaction kinetics.

1. **Elementary Reactions**: Individual steps in a reaction mechanism involving the collision of reactant molecules or ions to form products.
2. **Intermediate Species**: Transient species formed during the course of a reaction that are consumed in subsequent steps.
3. **Rate-Determining Step**: The slowest step in the reaction mechanism that determines the overall rate of the reaction.

Factors Affecting Reaction Rates

Several factors influence the rates of chemical reactions:

1. **Concentration of Reactants**: Higher concentrations of reactants generally lead to faster reaction rates, as there are more collisions between reactant molecules.
2. **Temperature**: Increasing temperature usually increases reaction rates by providing more kinetic energy to reactant molecules, leading to more frequent and energetic collisions.
3. **Catalysts**: Catalysts increase reaction rates by providing an alternative reaction pathway with lower activation energy, thereby lowering the energy barrier for the reaction.
4. **Surface Area**: In heterogeneous reactions, increasing the surface area of solid reactants enhances reaction rates by exposing more reactive sites.
5. **Pressure**: For gas-phase reactions, increasing pressure can increase reaction rates by reducing the average distance between gas molecules, leading to more frequent collisions.

Reaction Kinetics in Practice

1. **Experimental Techniques**: Various experimental techniques, such as spectroscopy, chromatography, and calorimetry, are used to measure reaction rates and elucidate reaction mechanisms.
2. **Kinetic Modeling**: Mathematical models, based on rate laws and reaction mechanisms, are used to simulate and predict reaction kinetics under different conditions.
3. **Process Optimization**: Reaction kinetics data are used to optimize reaction conditions, reactor design, and catalyst selection in industrial processes to maximize efficiency and yield.

Zero, Pseudo-Zero, First, and Second Order Reactions

Chemical reactions exhibit different kinetics depending on the rate at which reactants are consumed and products are formed. Zero, pseudo-zero, first, and second order reactions are common types of reactions categorized based on their rate laws and reaction kinetics. This content explores each of these reaction orders, their characteristics, and examples.

Zero Order Reactions

In a **zero order reaction**, the rate of the reaction is independent of the concentration of one or more reactants. The rate law for a zero order reaction is:

Rate=?Rate=k

where ?k is the rate constant.

1. **Characteristics**:

   - The rate of the reaction is constant over time.
   - The concentration of reactants does not affect the rate.
   - The reaction rate depends solely on the rate constant ?k.

2. **Examples**:

   - Decomposition of a stable molecule under constant conditions.
   - Enzyme-catalyzed reactions at high substrate concentrations where enzyme saturation occurs.

Pseudo-Zero Order Reactions

A **pseudo-zero order reaction** occurs when one reactant is present in such excess that its concentration remains essentially constant throughout the reaction, leading to a rate law that appears zero order with respect to that reactant.

1. **Characteristics**:

   - The rate law appears zero order with respect to the reactant present in excess.
   - The true order of the reaction may be different from zero order when considering the overall reaction mechanism.

2. **Examples**:

   - Catalytic reactions where the concentration of the catalyst remains constant.
   - Enzyme-catalyzed reactions at high substrate concentrations where the enzyme is not saturated.

First Order Reactions

In a **first order reaction**, the rate of the reaction is directly proportional to the concentration of a single reactant. The rate law for a first order reaction is:

Rate=[?]Rate=$k[A]$

where ?k is the rate constant and [?]$[A]$ is the concentration of the reactant.

1. **Characteristics**:

   - The rate of the reaction decreases exponentially over time as reactant is consumed.
   - The half-life of the reaction is constant.
   - The reaction rate depends linearly on the

concentration of the reactant.

2. **Examples**:

- Radioactive decay of isotopes.
- Decomposition of unstable compounds.

Second Order Reactions

In a **second order reaction**, the rate of the reaction is proportional to the square of the concentration of a single reactant or to the product of the concentrations of two different reactants. The rate law for a second order reaction is:

$$\text{Rate}=[?]2 \text{ or Rate}=?[?][?] \quad \text{Rate}=k[A]2 \text{ or Rate}=k[A][B]$$

where $?k$ is the rate constant and $[?][A]$ and $[?][B]$ are the concentrations of the reactants.

1. **Characteristics**:

- The rate of the reaction decreases as reactant is consumed or as the concentration of reactants decreases.
- The half-life of the reaction depends on the initial concentration of the reactant(s).
- The reaction rate depends on the square of the concentration of a single reactant or on the product of the concentrations of two different reactants.

2. **Examples**:

- Bimolecular reactions such as the reaction between two different molecules.
- Dimerization reactions where two identical

molecules combine to form a product.

Determination of Reaction Order

Determining the reaction order is a fundamental step in understanding the kinetics of a chemical reaction. The reaction order indicates how the rate of the reaction depends on the concentration of reactants. This information is crucial for predicting reaction rates, designing reaction conditions, and optimizing chemical processes. Several experimental methods are commonly used to determine the reaction order accurately.

Initial Rate Method

The initial rate method involves measuring the rate of the reaction at the beginning (i.e., the initial stage) under various initial concentrations of reactants. By conducting multiple experiments with different initial concentrations and monitoring the reaction rate, one can determine the reaction order with respect to each reactant.

1. **Procedure**:

   - Prepare solutions with different initial concentrations of reactants.
   - Initiate the reaction and measure the rate of the reaction at the initial stage.
   - Repeat the experiment for different initial concentrations of reactants.
   - Plot the initial rate versus the initial concentration for each reactant.
   - Determine the reaction order with respect to each reactant based on the slope of the plot.

2. **Interpretation**:

- If the rate is directly proportional to the concentration of a reactant, the reaction is first order with respect to that reactant.
- If the rate is independent of the concentration of a reactant, the reaction is zero order with respect to that reactant.
- If the rate is proportional to the square of the concentration of a reactant, the reaction is second order with respect to that reactant.

Half-Life Method

The half-life method involves measuring the time required for the concentration of a reactant to decrease by half (i.e., the half-life) at various initial concentrations. For first order reactions, the half-life remains constant regardless of the initial concentration, while for zero order reactions, the half-life increases with increasing initial concentration.

1. **Procedure**:

    - Measure the time required for the concentration of a reactant to decrease by half at different initial concentrations.
    - Plot the half-life versus the initial concentration of the reactant.
    - Determine the reaction order based on the constancy or variation of the half-life with the initial concentration.

2. **Interpretation**:

    - If the half-life is constant regardless of the initial

concentration, the reaction is first order with respect to that reactant.

- If the half-life increases with increasing initial concentration, the reaction is zero order with respect to that reactant.

Integrated Rate Laws

Integrated rate laws describe how the concentration of reactants changes with time for reactions of different orders. By comparing the experimental data with the integrated rate laws, one can determine the reaction order and rate constant.

1. **Procedure**:

   - Derive and solve the integrated rate law for the reaction of interest.
   - Plot the concentration of reactants versus time for different orders of reaction.
   - Determine the reaction order based on the linearity or non-linearity of the plot.

2. **Interpretation**:

   - For first order reactions, the plot of ln(concentration) versus time is linear.
   - For second order reactions, the plot of 1/concentration versus time is linear.
   - For zero order reactions, the plot of concentration versus time is linear.

Physical and Chemical Factors Influencing the Chemical Degradation of Pharmaceutical Products

The stability of pharmaceutical products is essential to ensure their safety, efficacy, and shelf life. Chemical degradation can significantly impact the quality and performance of pharmaceuticals. Various physical and chemical factors influence the degradation processes, posing challenges for formulation, manufacturing, storage, and distribution. This content explores the key factors contributing to the chemical degradation of pharmaceutical products.

Physical Factors

1. **Temperature**: Elevated temperatures can accelerate chemical degradation reactions by providing sufficient energy to overcome activation barriers. Storage at higher temperatures than recommended can lead to increased degradation rates and decreased shelf life.

2. **Humidity**: Moisture can facilitate chemical degradation through hydrolysis, oxidation, or other moisture-dependent reactions. Hygroscopic pharmaceuticals are particularly susceptible to moisture-induced degradation, leading to reduced stability and potency.

3. **Light Exposure**: Exposure to light, especially ultraviolet (UV) radiation, can induce photochemical reactions leading to degradation. Photolabile compounds, such as certain vitamins, antibiotics, and biologics, are particularly vulnerable to light-induced degradation.

4. **Oxygen**: Oxygen can promote oxidative degradation reactions, leading to the formation of reactive oxygen species and degradation products. Oxygen-sensitive pharmaceuticals, such as certain antioxidants and drugs containing unsaturated bonds, require special handling and packaging to minimize oxidation.

5. **pH**: The pH of the formulation can influence the

stability of pharmaceuticals, especially those susceptible to acid- or base-catalyzed degradation reactions. Maintaining the pH within a specific range is crucial to minimize degradation and ensure product stability.

Chemical Factors

1. **Hydrolysis**: Hydrolytic degradation involves the cleavage of chemical bonds by water molecules, leading to the formation of degradation products. Hydrolysis is a common degradation pathway for esters, amides, and other functional groups susceptible to nucleophilic attack.
2. **Oxidation**: Oxidative degradation reactions involve the transfer of electrons to oxygen molecules, resulting in the formation of reactive oxygen species such as peroxides and free radicals. Oxidation can cause degradation of pharmaceuticals containing susceptible functional groups, such as alcohols, aldehydes, and thiols.
3. **Isomerization**: Isomerization reactions involve the rearrangement of atoms within a molecule, leading to the formation of isomeric compounds. Isomerization can affect the stability and bioactivity of pharmaceuticals, especially chiral drugs, by altering their stereochemical configuration.
4. **Photodegradation**: Photodegradation occurs when pharmaceuticals undergo chemical reactions upon exposure to light, particularly UV radiation. Photochemical reactions can lead to the formation of reactive intermediates, photoproducts, and degradation of sensitive functional groups.
5. **Polymerization**: Polymerization involves the formation

of polymer chains from monomeric units, leading to the cross-linking and insolubilization of pharmaceutical formulations. Polymerization reactions can occur in certain drug delivery systems, excipients, or packaging materials, affecting product stability and performance.

Temperature, Solvent, Ionic Strength, Dielectric Constant, Acid-Base Catalysis, and Numerical Problems in Chemical Kinetics

Chemical kinetics is the study of the rates of chemical reactions and the factors that influence them. Temperature, solvent, ionic strength, dielectric constant, and the presence of acids or bases can significantly affect reaction rates. Additionally, understanding acid-base catalysis and solving numerical problems based on rate laws are essential aspects of chemical kinetics.

Temperature

Temperature plays a critical role in chemical kinetics. Increasing temperature generally increases the rate of reactions by providing more kinetic energy to reactant molecules, leading to more frequent and energetic collisions. The effect of temperature on reaction rate is described by the Arrhenius equation:

$$?=??–????k=Ae–RTEa$$

where:

- $?k$ is the rate constant,
- $?A$ is the pre-exponential factor,
- $??Ea$ is the activation energy,
- $?R$ is the gas constant, and
- $?T$ is the temperature in Kelvin.

Solvent and Ionic Strength

The choice of solvent can influence reaction rates by affecting the solvation of reactant molecules and the stability of intermediates. Polar solvents, such as water, can enhance the rates of ionization and solvation, whereas nonpolar solvents may slow down certain reactions. Ionic strength, determined by the concentration of ions in solution, can also affect reaction rates, especially for reactions involving charged species.

Dielectric Constant

The dielectric constant ($?\varepsilon$) of a solvent reflects its ability to reduce the electrostatic interactions between charged particles. Solvents with higher dielectric constants can stabilize charged species, facilitating ionization and enhancing reaction rates. The effect of dielectric constant on reaction rates is often described by the Debye-Hückel equation for ionic solutions.

Acid-Base Catalysis

Acid-base catalysis involves the presence of acids or bases that can donate or accept protons, thereby facilitating chemical reactions. Specific acid-base catalysis involves the participation of specific acids or bases in the reaction mechanism, while general acid-base catalysis involves the solvent or other constituents acting as acids or bases.

Simple Numerical Problems

Numerical problems in chemical kinetics often involve determining reaction rates, rate constants, and reaction orders based on experimental data. For example, given the initial concentrations of reactants and the corresponding reaction rates, one can use the initial rate method to determine the reaction order with respect to each reactant and calculate the rate constant. Additionally, numerical integration of rate laws can be used to predict the concentration of reactants or products at specific time points.

Stabilization of Medicinal Agents Against Common Reactions: Hydrolysis and Oxidation

Ensuring the stability of medicinal agents against common degradation reactions like hydrolysis and oxidation is crucial for maintaining their efficacy, safety, and shelf life. Pharmaceutical formulations must be carefully designed and optimized to minimize degradation pathways and enhance stability. This content explores strategies for stabilizing medicinal agents against hydrolysis and oxidation.

Hydrolysis

Hydrolysis involves the cleavage of chemical bonds by water molecules, leading to the formation of degradation products. Hydrolytic degradation is a common concern for pharmaceuticals containing ester, amide, or other hydrolyzable functional groups. Strategies to stabilize medicinal agents against hydrolysis include:

1. **Selection of Stable Functional Groups**: Choosing chemically stable functional groups that are less susceptible to hydrolysis, such as ethers instead of esters or secondary amides instead of primary amides.

2. **pH Adjustment**: Maintaining the pH of the formulation within a suitable range to minimize hydrolytic degradation. Buffering agents can be added to stabilize the pH and prevent acid- or base-catalyzed hydrolysis reactions.

3. **Protective Coatings or Encapsulation**: Coating medicinal agents with protective layers or encapsulating them in micro- or nano-scale carriers to shield them from direct contact with water molecules.

4. **Use of Hydrolysis Inhibitors**: Incorporating hydrolysis

inhibitors or stabilizers into the formulation to slow down or inhibit hydrolytic degradation reactions. Common inhibitors include antioxidants, chelating agents, and enzyme inhibitors.

Oxidation

Oxidation involves the transfer of electrons to oxygen molecules or other oxidizing agents, leading to the formation of reactive oxygen species and degradation products. Oxidative degradation is a major concern for pharmaceuticals containing susceptible functional groups such as alcohols, aldehydes, and thiols. Strategies to stabilize medicinal agents against oxidation include:

1. **Antioxidants**: Adding antioxidants such as tocopherols (vitamin E), ascorbic acid (vitamin C), or butylated hydroxyanisole (BHA) to scavenge free radicals and prevent oxidative degradation.
2. **Use of Oxygen Scavengers**: Incorporating oxygen scavengers or oxygen-absorbing materials into the packaging or formulation to reduce the oxygen concentration and minimize oxidative reactions.
3. **Selection of Packaging Materials**: Choosing packaging materials with low gas permeability to oxygen, such as amber-colored glass or aluminum foil, to protect medicinal agents from oxidation during storage and distribution.
4. **Storage Conditions**: Storing medicinal agents under inert atmospheres or in nitrogen-flushed containers to minimize exposure to oxygen and prevent oxidative degradation.

Accelerated Stability Testing in Expiration Dating of Pharmaceutical Dosage Forms

Accelerated stability testing is a crucial component of the pharmaceutical development process, particularly in determining the shelf life or expiration dating of pharmaceutical dosage forms. This testing helps predict the stability of drug products under accelerated storage conditions, enabling manufacturers to establish appropriate expiration dates. Additionally, photolytic degradation, caused by exposure to light, is a significant concern in pharmaceuticals. Understanding photolytic degradation mechanisms and implementing preventive measures are essential for ensuring product stability. This content discusses accelerated stability testing and strategies for preventing photolytic degradation in pharmaceutical dosage forms.

Accelerated Stability Testing

1. **Purpose**: Accelerated stability testing aims to evaluate the stability of pharmaceutical products over a shorter period by subjecting them to stress conditions, such as elevated temperature and humidity.

2. **Experimental Design**: The testing involves storing drug products under accelerated conditions, typically at higher temperatures (e.g., 40°C or 50°C) and humidity levels (e.g., 75% relative humidity) than those recommended for long-term storage. Samples are periodically analyzed for changes in physical, chemical, and microbiological properties.

3. **Evaluation Parameters**: Various parameters, including drug potency, degradation products, pH, dissolution rate, and microbial growth, are monitored to assess product stability. Accelerated degradation rates are

extrapolated to estimate shelf life under normal storage conditions.

4. **Regulatory Guidance**: Regulatory agencies, such as the FDA and EMA, provide guidelines for conducting accelerated stability testing and establishing expiration dates for pharmaceutical products. These guidelines outline the testing conditions, acceptance criteria, and documentation requirements.

Photolytic Degradation and Prevention

1. **Mechanisms**: Photolytic degradation occurs when pharmaceuticals are exposed to light, particularly ultraviolet (UV) radiation, leading to chemical reactions and degradation. Common mechanisms include photolysis of sensitive functional groups, oxidation, and formation of reactive intermediates.

2. **Preventive Measures**:

   - **Light-Protective Packaging**: Using opaque or amber-colored packaging materials to shield pharmaceuticals from light exposure during storage and distribution.
   - **Light Stabilizers**: Incorporating light stabilizers, such as UV absorbers or antioxidants, into formulations to mitigate the effects of photolytic degradation.
   - **Light-Blocking Excipients**: Adding light-blocking excipients, such as titanium dioxide or iron oxide, to formulations to reduce light penetration and protect sensitive drugs.
   - **Storage Conditions**: Storing pharmaceuticals in light-resistant containers and minimizing exposure

to direct sunlight or artificial light sources.

3. **Analytical Techniques**: Employing analytical methods, such as UV-visible spectroscopy, high-performance liquid chromatography (HPLC), or mass spectrometry, to detect and quantify photolytic degradation products and assess product stability.

* 9 7 9 8 8 9 4 4 6 2 3 5 6 *